Through
Five Hundred Years

A Popular History of the
Moravian Church

Allen W. Schattschneider

Drawings by Allie C. Blum

The Moravian Church in America
1021 Center Street, Bethlehem, Pa. 18018
500 South Church Street, Winston-Salem, N.C. 27101

Library of Congress Catalog Card Number: 89-69833

ISBN: 1-878422-01-4

Cover Design: Morgan Brooke

Printed in the United States of America

1991 2M

Contents

The Chalice Held High, For All to See

In times of bitter persecution members of the early Moravian Church met secretly, in the forest, to worship God. The chalice, used in the sacrament of Holy Communion, was a symbol of the Unitas Fratrum, forerunner of the modern Moravian Church. The Catholic Church denied the laity the right to drink from the chalice in communion.

Preface

This book first appeared in 1956 in time for the 500th anniversary celebrations of the Moravian Church in 1957. It quickly found a place in the homes of church members and as a textbook for use in confirmation classes. Minor updating was done in 1967 and a major revision was completed in time for a fifth printing in 1974. Now that another fifteen years have passed with significant changes in the nature of the worldwide Moravian Church, this third edition is published for current readers.

Allen W. Schattschneider was born in Bruderheim, Alberta, Canada, where his father was a pioneer pastor in the Canadian District of the Moravian Church. After public school education in North Dakota and Minnesota, he attended Moravian College and Moravian Theological Seminary, subsequently doing post-graduate work in Biblical (now New York) Theological Seminary, New York University, and the University of Pennsylvania. He holds doctor's degrees from Biblical and Moravian Seminaries. In 1961 he was consecrated a bishop of the Moravian Church.

His pastoral service began on Staten Island, New York, in 1925; in 1968 he retired from the pastorate of the Lititz, Pa., congregation and became teacher of the Bible courses in the Linden Hall School for Girls and subsequently served as chaplain of Moravian Manor at Lititz. His interest in Moravian history began with his teaching of the subject in youth camps and conferences in various areas of the Moravian Church in America.

This third edition was revised and prepared for publication by Albert H. Frank. A native of New Jersey, he was educated at Moravian College and Moravian Theological Seminary. Following mission service in the Eastern West Indies, he returned to stateside pastorates and did graduate work at the Lutheran Theological Seminary at Philadelphia and Drew University, from which school he holds the Doctor of Ministry degree. His lifelong interest in Moravian church history has involved teaching at Moravian Theological Seminary and authorship of several articles and book revisions.

A paragraph from the original preface written by John S. Groenfeldt is a good conclusion to this new preface: "This volume is offered to the church with the hope that it may be useful in giving both our young people and our adult members a deeper appreciation of the heritage which is ours and a better understanding of the faith which has been committed to us by our forefathers who loved and served the Lord in their day even as we seek to love and serve Him in our generation."

Chapter 1

From Bethlehem to Rome

The Story of One Life

The history of the Christian church begins in "the little town of Bethlehem," on a Christmas Eve long ago, when shining angels announced the birth of the Son of God, and humble shepherds hastened through the night to worship at his manger bed.

Not since time began have so many men and women told the story of one life. Every year produces new "lives" of Christ, but neither the most recent, nor the oldest, nor all of them together can tell everything about him who spoke as no person had ever spoken before, and whose ministry could be summed up in the words: "He went about doing good." The blind and the deaf and the lame felt the healing touch of his hands; "the common people heard him gladly"; and the little children climbed upon his knees.

No story in all the world has so touched the hearts of people as has the story of the way in which he died, and nothing that has happened in our world has so greatly cheered the human spirit as has the story of how he broke the chains of death and walked out of the tomb.

A gospel as glorious as the one which Christ put into the hearts of his disciples could not long be confined within the walls of old Jerusalem. Within a few months Philip had planted the gospel in Samaria, and within a few years Saul the persecutor, now Paul the Apostle, had taken the gospel all the way to Rome. Turn to the book of Acts and read the story of this man Paul; trace his "missionary journeys" on your maps. "Only three cubits in stature," Chrysostom wrote of him, "but he touched the sky!"

About the time Paul was put to death, the Roman historian Tacitus

admitted that the Christian faith, which he called "a pestilent superstition,".
. ."though checked for the time being," had "broken out afresh, not only in
Judea, where the mischief started, but also at Rome."

The Bitter Days of Persecution

Tacitus tells us also how Nero, accused of having set fire to the city of
Rome, turned aside the anger of the people by saying that the fires had been
started by the Christians. "A vast multitude were convicted," he writes. "In
their deaths they were made the subjects of sport, for they were covered with
the hides of wild beasts and worried to death by dogs or nailed to crosses or
set fire to. . .and burned to serve as lights at night. Nero offered his own
gardens for this exhibition."

During the first two centuries of the Christian era one persecution followed
another. The mad butchery of Nero was followed by systematic and cruel
efforts to stamp out Christianity. The chief crime of the Christians, in the eyes
of the Roman government, was the fact that they refused to worship the
Roman emperor. Such a refusal was looked upon as an act of rebellion. To
be a Christian was to be a traitor, and traitors deserved only to die. The
position of the Christians was made even more miserable by the fact that
every earthquake, every fire or calamity of any kind, was blamed upon them.
Such things, it was said, were signs of the anger of the gods because the
Christians were allowed to defy them.

We Fill Your Cities!

But neither systematic persecutions, not the throwing of Christians to the
lions for the entertainment of their enemies, nor inhuman torture, nor slander
and hatred, could stop the onward march of the faith. About the year 200
Tertullian, a Roman lawyer who had become a leader in the Christian church,
cried out, "We are but of yesterday, but we fill your cities!" Here and there
Christians cursed Christ in order to save their lives, but those who yielded to
this temptation were put to shame by the courage of countless hundreds in
every city who gave up their lives rather than deny their Lord. When the aged
Bishop Polycarp was told that if he would curse his Christ he would be
allowed to live, he replied: "Eighty and six years have I served him, and he has
done me nothing but good; how could I curse him, my Lord and Savior!"

So it came about at last that the Roman Empire, which had conquered the
world with the sword, was itself defeated by the followers of One who never
used a sword at all. The first "edict of toleration" came in 311 when Galerius
made Christianity a "permitted" religion, and urged Christians *to pray to their
God* for the emperor and the state. When Constantine became supreme ruler

of the West, his edict of toleration in 313 brought the long years of persecution to an end (with the exception of a few instances under later emperors).

With the ending of all restrictions the church began to push out boldly in every direction. Missionaries were sent to places as far away as England, where the gospel had been taken years before by the refugees from Rome (some say by Peter or Paul, or both; others by Joseph of Arimathea). Bishop Ulphilas went to the Goths who lived beyond the Baltic Sea in what we would call southern Russia. About 450 St. Patrick, as he has come to be called, went to Ireland to preach the gospel. He gathered hearers around him in the open fields. Soon he found a monastery on land contributed by some of his first converts. About 500 Clovis, king of the Franks, became a Christian. It is said of him that when he first heard the story of the cruel death of Jesus he cried out, "O that I had been there with my Franks!"

In the course of time missionaries planted the gospel in northern Africa and in places as far away as Armenia and the Scandinavian countries. Even Greenland and Iceland heard the story of Jesus from the lips of men who were determined to carry out the Lord's commission (Matthew 28:19).

The Gospel Comes to Moravia

In the year 863 two brothers, Cyril and Methodius, came from Constantinople to the little kingdom of Moravia in the heart of Europe. They were members of the Greek Church and were faithful and industrious missionaries. Up and down the land they went, instructing the people in the doctrines of the Christian faith and preaching "repentance and the remission (forgiveness) of sins." Cyril even invented an alphabet for the Moravians so that he and his brother could translate the Bible into their language. They organized congregations and trained young men to be priests. Best of all, they conducted their services in the language of the people. Missionaries sent from Rome had already begun to force the use of Latin upon the churches they established, in spite of the fact that very few of the persons to whom they preached could understand a single word of that language. Through this policy the people were kept in ignorance, so that the church might more easily impose its controls upon them. Cyril and Methodius, however, had grown up in Greece and been educated in Constantinople among people who still looked upon the preaching of the gospel in the language of the hearers as the chief work of the church. Their work "stood out in bright contrast to the system which Rome introduced wherever she gained a foothold" (de Schweinitz). Their work sowed the seeds of that deep love for the truth, that passionate insistence upon having the Word in one's own tongue, and that willingness to suffer and die for the faith which found expression, a few centuries later, among the followers of Master John Hus.

The Organization of the Early Church

The Christian church began as an organization in which all believers were looked upon as "brethren" (Matthew 23:8). The apostles were the natural leaders. They, in a sense, were the first "officers." Next came the "deacons" (Acts 6; 1 Timothy 3:8ff). As the church began spreading, "elders" were chosen to take charge of new congregations. Such men were frequently called "overseers" or "bishops." It was natural that in the course of time the bishops of the largest and most important congregations should have come to be looked up to by the smaller churches. It was natural, for instance, that a certain amount of prestige should attach itself to the office of the bishop of Jerusalem. His church was, after all, "the home church." We know from the book of Acts that Antioch soon became an important outpost; it was here that the disciples were first called "Christians" (Acts 11:26). The Antioch church was the first to send relief to the Christians in Judea when a famine came (Acts 11:27-30), and it was the Antioch church which, after fasting and praying, sent out Barnabas and Saul upon what became the first missionary journey (Acts 13:1-3). So the bishop of Antioch soon took his place beside the bishop of Jerusalem as a respected leader of the Christian church. After Paul had planted the gospel in Rome, which was still the political capital of the world, the bishop of that city soon assumed a place of importance. When the church spread into Egypt, Alexandria because of its great university and its large library soon became the "mother church" in Africa. Scholars like Clement and Origen helped the Alexandria church maintain its dignity and importance. When Constantinople was founded by Constantine, who made Christianity a favored religion in the empire, that city rapidly assumed a powerful position among the leading centers of the church.

In the year 451 the Council of Chalcedon recognized what had occurred, and ordered that the name "Patriarch" should henceforth be applied only to the bishops of Jerusalem, Antioch, Rome, Alexandria, and Constantinople.

One Against Four

A study of a map at this point will reveal an interesting and important fact: Of the five bishoprics recognized by the Council of Chalcedon, four were in the "East"; Rome was by herself in the "West." Centuries of strife and intrigue of every kind may be summed up in two sentences. In the East no one of the four bishops could long dominate the other three; the more they quarreled among themselves, the weaker each one became. In the West Rome had the field to herself and lost no opportunity for strengthening her position and increasing her power.

Papa Urbis Aeternae

In the year 404 the Roman Emperor Honorius moved out of Rome to the city of Ravenna, where his successors resided also. With the emperors out of the way, the bishop of Rome added to his title the phrase, "Papa Urbis Aeternae" (father of the eternal city). History soon gave the Roman bishop the opportunity he needed to establish his claims, for when Attila and the Huns began sweeping down into Italy in 451, it was the bishop of Rome, dressed in glorious robes, who went out bravely to meet him, and "by gold and persuasion," as the old historians put it, induced him to spare the city. Again in 455, when the Vandals threatened Italy, the Emperor remained in hiding at Ravenna while the Roman Bishop Leo I defied and dealt with the enemy.

The position of the bishop was greatly strengthened also by the publication, during these important years, of Augustine's great book *The City of God*. "The Roman Empire is falling," said Augustine. "What difference does it make? Let it fall! The Emperor is destined anyway to be replaced by the spiritual Head of the church. After all, Rome is God's city, not for political reasons, but because she is the capital of the Christian Church." With support like this, Leo I boldly advanced the claim that the bishop of Rome was the successor to Peter, chief of the apostles, and the vicar of Christ. Peter was the rock, said he, "which our Lord has wonderfully laid as the foundation." Leo's successors kept this claim alive, and reaffirmed it at every opportunity. Gregory I (550-604) called himself "the universal patriarch." While the four bishops in the East argued among themselves, and weakened each other in the process, the Roman bishops, many of whom were not only vigorous but capable leaders, lost no opportunity for increasing their power and prestige.

The greatest opportunity for strengthening the position of the bishop of Rome came in the year 800. The old Roman Empire had disappeared. In the north Charles Martel, king of the Franks, had decisively defeated the Moslems in 732 and the bishops of Rome were shrewd enough to realize that a new man of power had appeared upon the stage of history. For some years the bishops cultivated the friendship of Charles and his successors. Charles's son Pepin twice delivered Rome from the Lombards. In the year 800 Pepin's son Charles visited Rome. During the celebration of the mass on Christmas Day the bishop of Rome suddenly approached Charles, who was worshiping in St. Peter's, and crowned him "Emperor of the Romans." With characteristic boldness the bishop of Rome had seen his chance and taken it. By this bold act he roused the people of the entire West to loyalty and devotion to a new emperor. The fact that this new emperor owed his position to the bishop of Rome was all to the good. In the mind of the bishop of Rome this meant that the new empire and emperor, being the creation of the church, were therefore subject to it. From the empire she had created, it was logical for the church to expect obedience. "Jesus, the King of glory," wrote Gregory VII a few centuries later, "has made Peter lord over the kingdoms of this world." The church, as Innocent III expressed it, is the sun; the state is only the moon, which borrows its light from the sun.

Who Shall Rule?

That kings and emperors should have resented the arrogant claims of the popes, as the bishops of Rome came to call themselves, was only natural. At times the strife was due to the resentment of kings over the many ways in which the papacy interfered with the purely political affairs of their kingdoms. Upon other occasions it was the kings who in their struggles for power assumed the right to anoint men to positions in the church. Kings wanted this power because many bishops and abbots controlled vast wealth and owned great estates.

Probably the most famous battle between a pope and an emperor is that between Pope Gregory VII and King Henry IV. Henry was brave enough (as those of you who have read your history will remember) when he shouted at the Pope: "Get down! Get down!" but for all his boldness he ended up at Canossa, standing barefoot for three days in the winter of 1077 before the Pope even deigned to hear his pleas for pardon. He was able, it is true, to have his revenge upon Gregory a few years later when he succeeded in driving him into exile, but even the satisfaction of having defeated an old enemy could not wipe out the disgrace he had suffered. A Roman Emperor had been forced to submit completely to the bishop of Rome!

However, it was not only lust for worldly power which made the church inwardly weak and corrupt when she was outwardly so strong. There grew up also in the church a lust for wealth. In plain language, *gold* became more important than *God*.

"Silver and Gold Have I None"

It was the year 1254, and Pope Innocent IV lay dying in the papal palace in Rome. The ten years of his reign had been busy ones. He had fought a war with Emperor Frederick and crushed him. He had deposed the Emperor's son Conrad, when he entered Rome to ascend his father's throne. Now his bitter wars were over. Members of his family and a few friends stood around his bed. Suddenly Innocent lifted himself slightly and asked, "Why are you crying? Am I not leaving all of you rich?"

Innocent had indeed made his relatives and friends rich. The scholar Matthew of Paris had complained that Innocent was turning the papal court into a money changer's table, and the archbishop of Salzburg had been made angry enough to say publicly that "under the cloak of the shepherd there is to be seen, unless we are blind, the form of a ravenous wolf."

Nevertheless, the wealth which Innocent IV had accumulated by war and plunder and by openly selling to the highest bidder every office in the church, from that of a bishop down to that of a parish priest, was insignificant when compared with the wealth Pope John XXII acquired less than a century later. In order to forestall criticism John issued a papal bull in 1323, announcing that those who maintained that Christ and the disciples were poor were rebels and heretics. Having thus cleared the decks for action, he turned all the attention of his holy office to piling up gold. He enforced his demands for tribute from "the feudal states" of Naples, England, Sicily, and Italy. Every church office had its price, and when protests were made against such commercialization of spiritual offices, John replied that the fees charged were not for the offices themselves but for the labor involved in preparing the necessary documents. An army of tax collectors swarmed over Europe collecting the "freewill offerings" of the faithful. Every bishop visiting Rome to make his report to the Pope paid a handsome fee for this privilege. Every abbot who became the head of a monastery needed a letter of confirmation from the Pope. In 1302 when the newly elected Abbot of St. Alban's went to receive his confirmation, the trip cost him 10,340 florins (equivalent to about $25,000). If any openly objected to the demands of the Pope, they were promptly excommunicated, which meant that no one was allowed to give them so much as one meal until they publicly repented of their folly. Starvation has persuasive powers!

When he died in 1334 at the age of ninety, John XXII left an estate of eighteen million florins, and ornaments and jewels worth nearly half that amount. His entire fortune amounted, in American money, to about sixty million dollars. St. Peter had not been ashamed to confess, "Silver and gold have I none." John XXII, who regarded himself as Peter's successor, died as the richest man in all Europe.

"Not Without Witness"

Paul and Barnabas insisted long ago that God never leaves himself "without witness" (Acts 14:17). Always there is something or someone to stand for God and truth.

We must never forget that even during these centuries of which we have been thinking, centuries so filled with "wickedness in high places," there were always good men and women who took no part in the scheming and conniving of their leaders and who in their own communities endeavored to live as Christians. While the popes were warring with kings and hurling their curses at those who opposed them, gentle St. Francis went up and down the land, content to care for the sick and "do the work of an evangelist." Popes and bishops were busy piling up wealth for themselves. Francis and his friends, dressed in coarse gray tunics, took the oath of poverty and warmed themselves by "Brother Sun."

That simple and pure devotion to holy things was never completely stamped out was demonstrated also in many of the crusades. We may freely admit that many crusaders were mere adventurers in search of new thrills. The greater truth, however, is that the crusades could never have taken place at all if it had not been for the thousands upon thousands of unimportant men and women (and even children, as we know from the tragic story of the Children's Crusade) who looked upon their parts in the great movement as service rendered out of love for God. That even some of the leaders shared this passion must be evident to all who will read the story of good King Louis IX of France who died en route to Jerusalem, crying out in his fever, "I will enter into thy house, O Lord; I will worship in Thy holy sanctuary; I will glorify thy Name."

As the centuries passed, the days approached in which people like these, whose eyes had been opened to the worldliness and wickedness of so many leaders in the church, were to have the opportunity to speak out boldly for their faith. The time was coming when some of them were going to be called upon to give their lives in order that "the truth as it is in Christ Jesus" might be reestablished in the church.

Chapter 2

Master John Hus
and His Friends

Fighting Words

Tradition says that followers of John Hus were fond of singing a certain hymn just before their minister's sermon. It begins with the stanza:

The Word of God, which ne'er shall cease,

Proclaims free pardon, grace and peace,

Salvation shows in Christ alone,

The perfect will of God makes known.

When we sing these words expressing our conviction that salvation is the free gift of God to all who have faith in Jesus Christ, we do not realize that we are singing "fighting words." We forget that these words were written as a protest against the evil practice of the Catholic Church in selling the forgiveness of sins to those who paid money for slips of paper called "indulgences."

It was in the year 1411 that this custom was first introduced into Bohemia and Moravia. John XXIII had just become pope and his first important act was to call Europe to a was against King Ladislaus of Naples. Now wars cost money. In order to raise the necessary funds the pope did what previous popes had done: he offered forgiveness of sins to all who would participate in his "crusade" by purchasing indulgences.

Within a short time papal agents swarmed throughout Europe. Often they traveled in groups with advance agents to announce their coming and to set up stands for them in the town squares.

In May of 1412 Wenzel Tiem and company arrived in the ancient city of Prague with a bountiful supply of indulgences. Papal representatives presided over great chests which they placed in all the important churches. Soon the traffic was in full sway in every great church except one. The exception was Bethlehem Chapel, whose preacher was Master John Hus. Although called a chapel, Hus' church was a very large building, capable of holding 3,000 people. To the crowds which thronged his church John Hus cried out,

> A man can receive the pardon of his sins only through the power of God and by the merits of Christ. Let who will proclaim the contrary, let the pope or a bishop or a priest say, "I forgive thy sins, I absolve thee from their penalty, I free thee from the pains of hell"—it is all vain and helps thee nothing. God alone, I repeat, can forgive sins through Christ, and he pardons the penitent only.

Master John Hus

Who was this man who dared to defy the Pope? He was an unknown peasant's son, born in 1369, probably on July 6. His name seems to have come from the obscure village of Hussinetz, in which he was born. How much preliminary schooling he had, no one can say; but he had friends who believed in him, for when he was ready to go to the great University of Prague, his friends and neighbors helped to pay his fees. He was graduated in 1393 and took his master's degree in 1396. Two years later he was invited to become a lecturer in the university. In 1401 he was made dean of the philosophical faculty, and in 1402 he became rector of the university. How large the university was no one can say with certainty, as estimates of the number of students vary all the way from 7,000 to 30,000.

During his busy days as lecturer and administrator, Hus became more and more interested in theology. He became especially fond of the writings of John Wyclif, the courageous English reformer who had died in 1384. When Hus read Wyclif's bold assertions to the effect that even the pope was not to be obeyed when his commands were contrary to the Scriptures, he felt that the brave little Englishman had found a great truth. And, as Jan Herben, a modern Czech historian, puts it, "Once a Czech sets his teeth into a matter that is clear to him, nobody will ever tear him away from it."

In 1402 Hus requested ordination as a priest, and shortly thereafter he was chosen to be the preacher in Bethlehem Chapel. This building had been erected in 1391 by patriotic Czechs who had stipulated that the sermons preached in it must be not in the Latin which the Catholic leaders insisted upon, but in the Czech language of the people. Bethlehem Chapel thus became a rallying point for thousands of Czechs who were earnestly seeking to learn the truth which could make them free. "The Czech tongue," said Hus, "is as precious to God as the Latin!"

In his dual position as rector of the university and preacher in the great chapel, Hus soon became known throughout the little kingdom of Bohemia. The queen became a faithful worshiper in the chapel, and King Wenzel admired the courage of Hus so greatly that when papal agents began protesting against some of the things he was preaching, he ordered that "Master John Hus is to be allowed to preach the Word of God in peace."

But even the support of the king and the queen could not turn aside the anger of the church which smarted under the rebukes of the fearless preacher. In July 1410 Hus was placed under a "ban" forbidding him to preach. Shortly thereafter more than 200 volumes of Wyclif's writings were publicly burned in the city of Prague while church bells were rung throughout the city. In spite of this grim warning Hus continued his work. In June 1412 a public debate was held in the university. Thousands of Hus's friends mingled with the students, and when the debate ended a crowd of cheering students carried Hus to his home. Less than one month later the church struck the first blow in the bitter struggle which was to cost Hus his life.

Martyrs of Christ

On Sunday morning, July 10, 1412, priests throughout the city of Prague were urging the faithful to buy indulgences. In three churches open protest was made. In each church a man stood up, interrupted the priest, and cried out: "Priest, thou liest! We have heard better things from Master John Hus. These indulgences are a fraud!" The three men, all of them mechanics, who had probably agreed in advance to challenge the teachings of their church publicly, were immediately arrested, beaten, taken to the Council House, tortured upon the rack, and then condemned to death. Word of what was occurring spread rapidly throughout the city, and crowds of students, with Hus as their leader, began surrounding the Council House, begging that the sentence of death be cancelled. In alarm the magistrates appealed to Hus, promising him that if he would induce the mob to go home they would remit the death sentence. Hus then appealed to the crowds, and they began to disperse. As soon as most of the people and students had started home, the magistrates called a strong guard of soldiers and began taking the three men to the place of execution. Once more the alarm was given, and people began to block the streets leading to the place of execution. Suddenly a command rang out, and the three men were beheaded in the street.

In wild frenzy the helpless crowd roared out its anger. Men and women trampled upon one another in an attempt to dip their handkerchiefs in the blood of the martyrs. A band of students reverently lifted up the bodies of the mechanics and carried them to Bethlehem Chapel. There Hus buried them with all the rites of the church, crying out, "They are martyrs of Christ; they have given their lives for the truth!"

The Stones of Cursing

Soon the Pope's "excommunication" of John Hus arrived in Prague. It was a lengthy document which forbade anyone to give him food or drink or a place of refuge. Further decrees ordered that Bethlehem Chapel was to be destroyed, that Hus was to be seized and held prisoner, and that three stones were to be thrown against his house as a sign of the everlasting curse of the church. On October 2, 1412 a band of armed men invaded the service at Bethlehem Chapel and attempted to seize Hus while he was preaching. His faithful congregation forced the men to leave the church. Bethlehem Chapel was watched day and night by friends ready to given an alarm, but no very serious attempt was ever made to destroy it. In an attempt to prevent further trouble King Wenzel asked Hus to withdraw from the city for awhile. Hus reluctantly agreed to his royal friend's request. During his "exile" he put down in writing expositions of the faith for which he was fighting. The most notable work of this period is *The Church*. In this volume, which he sent to Prague to be read in Bethlehem Chapel, Hus asserted that Christ alone was the true Head of the church, that the true church needed neither cardinals nor Pope, that even a Pope "through ignorance and the love of money" may make mistakes, and that to rebel against an erring Pope is to obey Christ.

On to Constance

In October 1413 Pope John XXIII issued the call for a council of the church to deal with abuses and to decide once and for all who was the true Pope. For thirty-five years there had been at least two "Popes," each one claiming to be the supreme head of the church on earth, and hurling curses at his rival. The common people had long protested against sad conditions like these. At last their protests had become loud enough to make an impression upon John XXIII.

When the call to this council, scheduled to be held in Constance, arrived in Bohemia, Prince Sigismund, who had now assumed many of the duties of his aged father, King Wenzel, suggested that Hus should go and plead his cause. When Hus's friends protested loudly that he ought not to go "into the camp of the enemy," Sigismund gave him a "safe conduct" reading,

> The honorable Master John Hus we have taken under the protection and guardianship of ourselves and of the holy empire. We enjoin upon you (that is, upon anyone who might think of harming him) to allow him to pass, to stop, to remain and to return, freely and without any hindrance whatsoever; and you will, as in duty bound, provide for him and his, whenever it shall be needed, secure and safe conduct, to the honor and dignity of our majesty.

Accompanied by two barons, Hus set out for Constance. Upon his arrival on November 3, 1414, he took lodgings in a home near the White Pigeon Inn. His two friends arranged to see the Pope, who assure them that Hus would not be harmed during his stay in the city. (The Pope's words were: "Even if he had killed my own brother. . .he must be safe while he is at Constance.")

Several weeks later Hus was summoned to a meeting with the cardinals. When he appeared, he was surrounded by soldiers and taken to a prison cell in a dungeon under the Dominican convent. The cell was right next to the sewer system, and Hus soon became violently ill. To his keeper Robert he gave a letter which eventually got back to Bohemia. "I am in prison and in chains," he wrote. "Keep me in remembrance and pray God that he may bestow faithfulness upon me and Jerome, my brother in Christ, for I believe that he will suffer death with me."

When it seemed as if Hus might die before the synod got around to considering his case (the synod actually lasted four years, so no one was in a hurry about anything), Hus was taken out of the foul dungeon and transferred to a kind of cage at the top of one of the towers of the castle of the Bishop of Constance. Here he had scant shelter from either the burning sun or the chilling night winds. For more than two months he was kept in this place, and every night his arm was chained to the wall so that he could not even try to keep warm by moving around.

Meanwhile "the Holy Synod of Constance," as it called itself in its resolutions, dragged on from month to month. Old records state that at least 50,000 people were present, including hundreds of buglers and fiddlers who had come to entertain the crowds. To thousands of the attendants the synod was no more significant than a country fair would be today.

When word of what had happened to Hus reached Bohemia, 250 noblemen signed a vigorous protest, demanding that "the beloved master and Christian teacher" be tried promptly and permitted to return home. This appeal was completely ignored. One of the barons who had accompanied Hus to Constance appealed directly to Prince Sigismund. Hus should be set free, but when the wily cardinals replied that it was not necessary to keep promises made to heretics, Sigismund said no more.

One June 5, 1415, Hus was taken out of prison and brought into the council. Into the details of the two trials, which lasted for a month, we cannot go. When Hus attempted to read from his book *The Church*, members of the examining commission drowned out his voice by shouting, "Burn the book! Burn the book!" When he declared that God and conscience were on his side, his examiners ignored his appeal to God and shouted, "We cannot go by your conscience."

"Today in His Kingdom"

On the morning of July 6 Hus was ushered into the cathedral. There sat Prince Sigismund, who had been false to his solemn promises of protection. There were the cardinals and bishops in their glorious robes. Hus was placed upon a hugh stool in the middle of the huge building. The Bishop of Lodi preached a funeral sermon saying that the blotting out of heretics was one of the works most pleasing to God. Thirty charges of heresy were read, and when Hus attempted to speak he was ordered to remain silent. The vestments of a priest were hung upon his shoulders and a communion cup was placed in his hands. Then the priestly garments were removed one by one and the communion cup was torn from his fingers with the words, "We take from thee, thou Judas, this cup of salvation!"

This time the reply of Hus could be distinctly heard: "But God does not take it from me, and I shall drink of it today in his Kingdom."

At length the proceedings came to an end. Attendants placed upon Hus's head a tall fool's cap decorated with a picture of three devils fighting for his soul, and the march to the place of execution began. A thousand soldiers cleared the way. As the procession passed the city square, Hus saw the huge bonfire in which copies of his books were being burned. Aeneas Sylvius, who later became Pope Pius II, admits that "not a word escaped him which gave indication of the least weakness." Over the bridge went the procession to an open field outside the city. Here a post had been firmly driven into the ground. To this stake Hus was bound with wet ropes. Then straw and wood were piled up around him. Once more he was asked if he would recant. "I shall die with joy," he replied, "in the faith of the gospel which I have preached."

An officer clapped his hands, and the burning torch was applied to the straw. As the flames flared up around him, Hus began to sing in Latin one of the chants of the church: "Christ, Thou Son of the Living God, have mercy upon me!" And so, upon "a chariot of fire" the soul of John Hus went up to heaven.

When the fire had consumed the martyr's body, soldiers gathered up the ashes and tossed them into the Rhine, so that friends might find nothing which could be kept as a relic of the man. A few of his countrymen came, nevertheless, when the soldiers had gone away, and dug up a bit of the ground where the stake had been planted and carried the ground all the way back to Bohemia with them.

Jerome of Prague, a nobleman who had come to Constance to plead for Hus before the Council, was seized while journeying back to Bohemia, dragged to Constance, condemned to death, and burned on the same spot on May 30, 1416. Today there stands upon this spot an ivy-covered boulder upon which are engraven the names of Hus and Jerome and the dates upon which they died.

Dangerous Anger

Hus's friends came home from Constance with heavy hearts and deep, silent, dangerous anger burning in their breasts. Everywhere they told the story of the deceit and treachery Hus had encountered and of how he had

been burned to death. The first result was a great increase in the number of the "Hussites," as they now called themselves. Throughout the land many persons who had paid little attention to the entire controversy now came out openly on the side of the reformer. An angry crowd stormed the palace of the Archbishop of Prague, forcing him to flee for his life. On September 2, 1415, no less than 420 barons and knights, all of them members of the Bohemian Diet, signed a letter of angry protest to the Council of Constance and three days later a "Hussite League" was formed.

The Council of Constance, as if in answer to the angry Bohemians, issued a threatening letter to the Bohemian nation and ordered the bones of John Wyclif dug up and burned.

Since they were now denied the use of church buildings, the Hussites began meeting in open fields. A great hill called Mount Tabor became one of

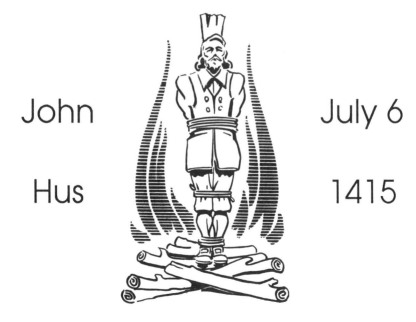

John

Hus

July 6

1415

their rallying points. Here on July 22, 1419, they held a great communion service to which thousands of Hussites came from every corner of the little kingdom. Old writers report that 40,000 persons were present. Many groups carried homemade banners with pictures of the communion cup upon them. The Catholic Church denied people the right to drink from the cup at communion, and since the Hussite priests not only served the bread, but also passed the cup to all who came in faith, it was natural that the communion cup should have become a Hussite symbol.

Less than two weeks after this great outdoor communion service the Hussite War broke out.

Lion-hearted Ziska

On July 30, 1419, there was a Hussite procession in the city of Prague. John of Selan, a former monk who had forsaken the monastery, was leading the group. As they passed the Council House where the council was in session, someone threw a stone at John. Immediately the Council House was stormed by the angry crowd. Eleven of the eighteen members escaped; the others were seized and thrown out of the windows of the council chamber onto the spears of the frenzied crowd below. News of the riot was sent to King Wenzel, who became so angry that he suffered a stroke and died shortly thereafter.

Prince Sigismund was not in Bohemia at the time, and he knew better than to come home. Like many another, he felt that "might is right," so he persuaded the Pope to proclaim a crusade against the rebellious Bohemians. "Thus began," Bishop de Schweinitz once wrote, "one of the most remarkable, and at the same time terrific wars the world has seen. For sixteen years Bohemia single-handed defied all of Europe."

Leader of the Hussites was John Ziska, "one of the greatest captains who had hitherto appeared in Europe." He was sixty-six when the war began, and blind in one eye, but his one good eye was worth more than all the eyes of his enemies. Riding into the heart of a battle upon a rude wagon, he directed his peasants, armed at times only with homemade weapons, pitchforks and clubs, against the trained soldiers of the emperor. From behind a barricade of wagons his followers would rush upon the enemy with long hooks with which they pulled soldiers out of their saddles. Ziska himself composed the Hussite battle hymn, "Ye who the Lord God's warriors are," and shouting these words his men ran to battle for their humble homes and their holy faith. In a proclamation to the citizens of a village named Tausch he wrote: "Let us have constantly before our eyes the Divine Law and the common good, and let whoever knows how to handle a knife or throw a stone or brandish a cup be ready to march! The hand of God is not shortened. Courage, therefore— and be ready!"

On July 14, 1420, at a place ever since called Ziska Hill, the Hussite armies defeated Sigismund's army of more than 100,000 soldiers. In August of 1421 there came a second "crusade" against the Hussites; in 1422 a third "crusade." Both ended in Hussite triumphs. In 1422 brave Ziska lost the sight of his good eye in battle, but even in his blindness he continued to direct his armies. For two years more he led his troops; then, on October 11, 1424, he was killed while he and his followers were storming an enemy stronghold. An old story says that after he died his soldiers carefully removed a piece of his skin and made a drum head out of it, so that even though he was no longer with them Ziska's drum might stir their hearts and terrify their enemies.

Next leader of "Ziska's Orphans," as the soldiers now called themselves, was a former priest who had joined the Hussites. His name was Prokop. He was not as great a military genius as Ziska, but he had a fearless heart. Even when the emperor sent 130,000 trained soldiers against the Hussites, Prokop and his friends completely defeated them. Then, when it seemed as if the Hussites could not be defeated by Pope and emperor, they defeated themselves by quarreling with one another.

Divide and Conquer

For some years there had really been two "parties" among the Hussites. The one group called themselves Utraquists. That word came from the Latin *sub utraque* ("under both kinds") and referred to their insistence upon partaking of both the bread and the cup in holy communion. The Utraquists kept suggesting that the differences between the Catholics and the Hussites were not as great as they were said to be and with a little giving in on each side, some kind of an agreement could surely be worked out. The second group, called Taborites (from Mount Tabor) realized how very great the differences between the Hussites and the Catholics actually were. They knew also that the Catholic Church would never do any "giving in" and was not sincerely interested in purifying itself. They pointed to the fact that the Council of Constance, which had been called for the very purpose of reforming the church, had lasted for four years, and then adjourned after an announcement by Pope Martin V to the effect that reforms would be postponed until the next council! The Catholic Church, said they, will never acknowledge that she has made any errors; she is certainly not interested in correcting abuses; she is interested only in crushing those who oppose her—what happened to John Hus ought to be proof enough of that. To arguments such as these the Utraquists only replied, "Don't be so unreasonable!"

And so it came about that the Pope, when he saw that his armies could not conquer the Hussites, resorted to another prescription: Divide and conquer. When Cardinal Julian proposed that he might get a really large group of Hussites to agree to a conference, the Pope immediately made plans for a meeting to be held at Basle. There they were received with studied kindness, and for two months the Catholics permitted a free and frank discussion of all points over which so much blood had been shed. The Catholics even listened without interruption to speeches in which John Hus was praised as a witness to the truth. "See," said the Utraquists, "the Catholics are reasonable after all. Surely we can made peace with them."

The Battle of Lipan

In the course of time an agreement known as the Compactata of Basle was signed, and Catholics and Utraquists went home rejoicing. The Taborites cried out loudly that the blood of John Hus had been shed in vain. Their protests were soon silenced. In anger the Utraquists turned upon them. raised an army, and with backing of the Catholics, announced that they would force the Taborites to submit. Prokop and his followers gathered themselves together. On May 30, 1434, the army of Catholics and Utraquists warriors fell upon them. When the sun went down on the evening of the bitter battle, Prokop and 13,000 of his warriors lay dead upon the fields of Lipan.

The battle of Lipan brought the Utraquists into a place of great power in Bohemia. John Rokycana, one of their leaders, became Archbishop of Prague. Soon overtures were made to Sigismund. In July 1436 a great meeting was held in the market place at Iglau at which Sigismund, who had fought so bitterly against the Hussites, was acknowledged to be king of Bohemia. At the same time the Bohemians were invited to return to the Catholic Church. Many accepted the invitation, although the Utraquist Church continued to exist for several centuries. The defeated and discouraged Taborites were driven into the underground.

Still Small Voice

But the cause for which Hus died, and for which Ziska and Prokop and thousands of their followers had given their lives was not yet lost. Within a few years John of Rokycana, the Utraquist Archbishop of Prague, was preaching against abuses in the Catholic Church. He sounded like John Hus come to life again! Even the Utraquists, said he, were falling into the same errors. Among those who rallied around Rokycana was his nephew Gregory, formerly a monk. When Rokycana cried out one Sunday that the priests by their wickedness had put the devil into the very elements of the holy communion, Gregory and his friends went to him asking, "What shall we do then? Will you lead us out of this wickedness into the truth?" Rokycana hesitated. He was brave enough to denounce wickedness from his pulpit, especially since that kind of preaching filled his church, but to be asked to suffer for his faith was another matter. At length he said to Gregory, "Go to Peter Chelchicky; he will help you."

Who was Peter Chelchicky? An humble farmer who patiently plowed his fields and asked himself again and again: "Why all this war and bloodshed? Why are fields like mine being destroyed all over the land? What about the commandment 'Thou shalt not kill'? Can wars bring in the kingdom of God?" In the course of time the humble thinker began to put his thoughts down in writing. It was some of these writings which had fallen into the hands of Rokycana.

An old history, written in 1547, tells us what happened: "Master Rokycana showed to the brethren Gregory and his friends writings of Peter Chelchicky, admonishing them to read these books which he himself read frequently. . .obeying his advice the brethren read the writings of this man with much diligence and had even many talks with him. . .from which they obtained much knowledge about the right way of life."

The direct result of these talks was the establishment of the Moravian Church. It came about when Gregory and his friends decided to establish a little community of their own in which they might endeavor to live out their Christian faith. Rokycana agreed to find a place for them and after consulting King George he obtained permission for the little group to settle on the estate surrounding the castle of Lititz.

To this quiet spot Gregory and his friends made their way. Near a little village called Kunwald they built humble homes. Soon other Hussites who had become weary of war and bloodshed joined them. Michael Bradacius, the priest of a neighboring village, left his church and joined them. He and Gregory were soon made the leaders of the group. Simple rules based upon the Bible were drawn up to govern the colony. "Let us call ourselves a Unity of Brethren," they said. The Bohemian phrase is *Jednota Bratrska*, a title that is still used by groups of Moravians who speak the Czech language, such as the Czech Moravian Brethren in Texas. The Latin form is *Unitas Fratrum*, and that form is used in many legal documents as the name of the Moravian Church.

The exact date upon which the Brethren formally organized their group is unknown. The year was 1457 and an old tradition fixes the date as March 1. Thus sixty years before Luther began his Reformation, the world's first Protestant church was born. Through five centuries the church lives on in spite of every effort to destroy it and is today the Moravian Church, a world-wide Unity of Brethren.

Did Peter Chelchicky live to see the day? No one can tell; one record says he died in 1455; another says he lived until 1460. Whether or not he lived to see the growth of the seed he had sown, "his works follow him." Even today we honor him who once summed up his teachings in these words: "I have learned from Christ, and by Christ I will stand."

Chapter 3

"Through Peril, Toil, and Pain"

The King Who Wanted to be Emperor

Although King George actually owned the Lititz estate upon which the Brethren had established their first settlement, he paid very little attention to the growing community. He had another matter on his mind, a plan for making himself emperor of the Holy Roman Empire. This empire included almost all of western Europe, and Bohemia was only one of the kingdoms in it.

King George believed that his chances for obtaining this honor were good. Emperor Frederick was neither very strong nor very popular, and prominent persons in other kingdoms were saying openly that George of Bohemia would make an excellent emperor. Even more important was the fact that the pope, who made and unmade emperors in those days, had visited Bohemia and obviously liked the Bohemian king. "Don't you see," George's friends said to him, "it would be a clever move on the part of Pope Pius to get rid of Frederick and make you the emperor. That would make the pope popular in Bohemia and that is just what he wants, for he is anxious to appease the Bohemians and get more of them back into the Catholic Church. Keep in well with the pope and you will be emperor before long."

King George thought this was good advise and made up his mind to follow it. His open desire to please the pope gave the enemies of the Brethren the chance for which they had been waiting. A group of them went to see the king. "Do you know," they asked him, "that the group of people whom you allowed to settle on your estate at Lititz several years ago are really heretics of the worst kind? What will the pope say if he hears that you actually permit such people to live on your land?"

King George was alarmed. Why had he ever listened to Rokycana? No heretics, said he to himself, are going to spoil things for me just when everything is working out so well. Straightway he issued an edict commanding all his subjects to join either the Catholic or the Utraquist Church. The enemies of the Brethren wasted no time in making use of the edict. Hearing that quite a number of students in the university had joined the hated Hussites, they began an "inquiry" into the life of the students at Prague. When we remember that "inquiry" and "inquisition" come from the same root, we see what they had in mind.

"Follow Me to Prison"

At about the time the inquiry was begun, Gregory was in Prague visiting students who belonged to the Brethren. An evening meeting was arranged in a private home in the city. Just before the meeting a message was sent to Gregory (some think by his uncle Rokycana) warning him not to go to the meeting. Gregory felt that it would not be right for him to flee without warning the students, so he went to the home and suggested that everyone should go to his rooms in the university. The students laughed at him—they were not afraid of persecution. When Gregory tried to speak of what had happened to Master John Hus, some of the students boasted, "We'll have torture for breakfast and stake for dinner!"

Scarcely had they shouted their defiance when a magistrate entered the room with his men. He had no heart for the task to which he had been assigned; he looked at the little group and said, "All that will live godly lives must suffer persecution (2 Timothy 3:12). You must come with me to prison."

In prison the students were stretched out one by one upon a rack. The rack was like a cot with a heavy roller at each end. The victim's hands were tied to one roller and his feet to the other. Then strong men turned the rollers until arms and legs were pulled out of joint. The boastful students screamed that they would recant. An early historian writes of them that "after having tasted of their breakfast, they had no appetite for their dinner."

Then came Gregory's turn. Not until he had fainted away under the torture and seemed to be dead did his tormenters cease their work. Meanwhile someone had sent word to Rokycana of what was happening. Rushing into the place of torture, he began to wring his hands and cry out, "Oh, my

Gregory, my Gregory, if only I were dead!" Turning upon the torturers he shouted, "Unloose him, unloose him, do something for him!" Some one brought strong smelling salts. Poor Gregory shivered and moaned in his pain. At last he opened his eyes. "I have had a dream," he whispered. "I saw a beautiful tree in a meadow. The tree was covered with fruit and beautiful birds were carrying the fruit away. In front of the tree I saw Jesus standing, and in the meadow, watching over the tree, were three men whose faces I seem to know. I shall never forget them."

Rokycana succeeded in having Gregory released, but he refused to help other members of the group. Michael Bradacius was thrown into a dungeon, and soldiers drove the settlers out of their peaceful valley. At a place called Richenburg four of Gregory's friends were seized and burned to death. From their hiding places the Brethren appealed to Rokycana: "Have we deserved the persecutions you have brought upon us?" The archbishop made no reply and the persecutions continued. At last the Brethren spoke out plainly to Rokycana. "Thou art of the world," they wrote him, "and wilt perish with the world." But these bold words only increased the anger of Rokycana.

The Permanent Organization

The first persecution of the Brethren had two immediate results. In the first place it produced an increase in the membership of their group. Several priests joined their fellowship and other friends now openly allied themselves with Gregory and his friends. Here and there wealthy landowners secretly invited the Brethren to settle on their estates.

In the second place, persecution showed clearly that the only thing for the Brethren to do was to establish themselves as an independent Christian church. In 1464 a synod was held somewhere in the Bohemian mountains at which a statement of faith was issued, and three elders were elected as a governing board. Rokycana's suffragan bishop, Martin Lupac, suggested that the Brethren establish their own ministry. For giving this advice he lost his position and came to the Brethren. But he was soon caught and thrown into prison. In 1467, shortly before he died, Martin saw his advise bear fruit, for at a synod held in that year three men were chosen to be ministers of the Brethren: Matthias, Thomas, and Elias. Before the choice was made, Gregory, who was president of the synod, lifted up his scarred and twisted hands in prayer. When the three men had been chosen, he cried out, "These are the men whose faces I saw in the dream I had as I lay upon the rack."

The next question was who was to ordain the new ministers. Many priests had joined the Brethren, but they had no bishops. It was suggested that all the former priests should ordain the new ministers. This was done, but in order to make sure that their ministers would have to be recognized even by their enemies, it was decided that ordination by a bishop should be sought.

Obviously no Catholic or Utraquist bishop would help, so the Brethren turned to an aged Waldensian bishop named Stephen. The Waldensians were an independent society of Christians, not completely Protestant as we use the word today and yet refusing to accept certain Catholic doctrines as, for instance, belief in purgatory. At times the Catholics tolerated them; at other times they were bitterly persecuted, especially in later years as they became more and more Protestant in their views. When the Brethren turned to them in 1467, they had several priests who had been consecrated bishops by Catholic bishops, so they had an order of bishops which even the Catholics recognized. Bishop Stephen and another Waldensian bishop, whose name has been lost, listened with interest to the request of the Brethren. Then he and his colleague consecrated the aged Michael Bradacius the first bishop of the Brethren. When he returned home after his visit to Bishop Stephen, Michael consecrated Matthias a bishop, and so the order of bishops began in our church and has continued to this day.

Pre-Reformation Days

Kind-hearted Bishop Stephen soon learned how dangerous it was to help those whom the Catholic Church hated, for in 1469 he was seized, taken to Vienna, and put to death. In 1473 stout-hearted Gregory died in the little house he had built for himself in Kunwald Valley.

The next great leader of the Brethren was Luke of Prague. He had been brought up as a member of the Utraquist Church and a graduate of the University of Prague. When he joined the Brethren, he found that quite a controversy was going on among them over the value of education. Some of the leaders of the Brethren were very much afraid that education would draw people away from the truth. Even Gregory had been firmly convinced of this. It is said that his dying words were, "Beware of the educated brethren." But Luke and his friends argued that John Hus had been a highly educated man, and that education could be used to further the cause of Christ. In 1500 Luke was consecrated a bishop and for many years this brilliant and devoted man exercised a great influence upon the Brethren's Church.

In 1502 Bishop Luke published his first *Catechism for Children*. This little book went through one edition after another. After Luther's Reformation began (in 1517) Bishop Luke's catechism was translated into German. It was circulated widely throughout Germany and helped the cause of Protestantism there. Bishop Luke also had a great deal to do with the publication of the first Protestant hymnbook, issued by the Brethren in 1501. This book contained eighty-nine hymns, some of which Luke had written, others were by John Hus and some were Bohemian versions of ancient Latin hymns. In the Catholic Church only the priests sang or chanted, usually in Latin. In the Brethren's Church the people were encouraged to sing their faith in their own language. Bishop Luke introduced liturgies and chants and encouraged congregations to make their church buildings as attractive as they could.

The Reformation in Germany

We cannot tell here the inspiring story of Martin Luther and the way in which he, as John Hus had done a hundred years before, defied the pope and led the people of Germany back to the faith of the New Testament. We can only mention the fact that the Brethren in Bohemia rejoiced greatly when news of the Reformation reached them. Bishop Luke sent Luther a letter of encouragement, and in 1522 the Brethren John Horn and Michael Weiss were sent to visit Luther. In 1524 they made a second visit, and for years there were numerous contacts between the Brethren and the Lutherans. In 1538 Luther printed a confession of faith for the Brethren and paid them a high tribute in an introduction he wrote for the little volume.

In Germany, in spite of the opposition of Emperor Charles, the Reformation continued to make progress. At last, chiefly because Charles's rival, the king of France, promised to help the Protestants if they went to war, Charles was forced to make peace with the Protestants. The treaty was called the Peace of Augsburg. It was signed in 1555 and gave each prince the right to determine the faith of his subjects. While this was scarcely the best way to settle the issue, it did give Protestants some chance to live in peace. What happened was that within a short time the northern half of Germany was almost solidly Protestant while the southern portions of the country remained Catholic.

Within Six Weeks

In Bohemia, however, the Protestants had no chance at all to establish themselves. In this unhappy little kingdom Ferdinand I had come to the throne. For a few years he made no open attack upon the Brethren; then came the "Smalcald War" in which Frederick of Saxony rallied the Protestants to fight against the Catholics. King Ferdinand now ordered the Bohemian people to rally around him and assist in defending the kingdom against the Protestant rebels. The Brethren were in a most unhappy position. They did not want to be disloyal to their king, but if they fought with him they would be going to war against fellow Protestants. The great majority of them refused to take any part in the war; others defied their own king and went or sent help to the Protestant leader.

On April 24, 1547, the great battle of Muhlberg was fought in which Frederick was defeated. Ferdinand came back to Bohemia flushed with his triumph and determined to punish those who had not rallied around him. In vain the Brethren argued that only a few of their number had openly opposed him. Ferdinand only snarled that the Brethren would either become Catholics or leave his country within six weeks.

That anyone would prefer his faith to his country seemed impossible to Ferdinand. But before many days had passed, several thousand members of the Brethren's Church were on their way to the neighboring kingdom of

Poland. Although branded enemies of the kingdom by Ferdinand, one town after another sent guards with them. They were excused from payment of road and bridge tolls and everywhere the people through whose lands they passed turned out to help them get their wagons over difficult places. As they went they sang the Hussite stanza:

Blest be the day when I must roam
Far from my country, friends and home,
An exile, poor and mean.
My fathers' God will be my Guide,
Will angel guards for me provide,
My soul, my soul in danger screen.

Ostrorog in Poland

George Israel, a blacksmith's son, was their leader. Working in his father's shop had given him muscles of iron, and the big man feared no one. While seeking a refuge for the Brethren, he and a few friends came one day to the great castle of the Count of Ostrorog, located just across the Polish border. The count was not at home, but the countess welcomed the little group, who offered to conduct a service in the castle. Shortly after Matthias Cerwenka had begun his sermon, the count arrived at home. Informed of what was happening, he stormed into the room, horsewhip in hand, shouting that he would have no heretics under his roof. Cerwenka went on preaching. George Israel stood up, glared at the blustering count, and, pointing to a chair, said, "Sir, sit down there!" The count obeyed, sat down, and began to listen. In a few moments his heart was touched by Cerwenka's simple gospel message. When the service ended, he announced that the Brethren whom these visitors represented would be welcome on his estates. Soon Ostrorog became the center of the Brethren in Poland, with the count as their most loyal supporter. In a few years no less than forty Brethren's congregations had been established in Poland.

"I Nominate Myself"

Although thousands of the Brethren left Bohemia because of Ferdinand's cruel edict, other thousands remained on the country, living as best they could. Here and there they found refuge upon the estates of noblemen who did not try very hard to enforce the king's decree. Always, however, they lived under the watchful eye of their enemies. One word spoken at the wrong time could mean imprisonment and possible death. But in the providence of God these bitter years produced a leader capable of encouraging his brethren, suffering with them, keeping them true to their faith. His name was John Augusta.

It was in 1532, when he was thirty-two years of age, that Augusta came into a position of leadership in the Brethren's Church. How did it happen? He nominated himself! A synod of the Brethren had been called to elect bishops and members of the Elders' Council (the governing board). John Augusta rose and addressed the members of synod. It was time, said he, that "new blood" was brought into the church. "The Council of Elders does not understand the needs of our day." He ended his speech by nominating himself and four other younger men for membership on the Council. Some of the members of synod were shocked at such impertinence, but when the votes had been counted it was found that Augusta and his four friends had been elected. What is more, Augusta and two other friends were consecrated bishops! Augusta, by reason of his boundless energy and his great gifts for leadership, soon became the unofficial "head" of the church. His fame spread far and wide, for he was a brilliant preacher. He visited both Luther and Calvin and gained their friendship and respect. In fact, shortly before he died, Luther sent a letter "to the venerable brother in Christ, John Augusta, my very dear friend."

The Martyr Bishop

Although he was astonished when thousands of the Brethren left his kingdom rather than become Catholics, Ferdinand continued his policy of bitter enmity against them. The presence of John Augusta in his kingdom made him furious. When he found that the mayor of Leitomischel would be glad to undertake the capture of the defiant bishop in return for a few favors from the king, he authorized Mayor Schoeneich to lay a trap for Augusta.

Schoeneich went to persons whom he thought to be Brethren and suggested that if he could only talk to Augusta he could tell him some things which might make life easier for the Brethren. When this news reached Augusta he offered to meet Schoeneich provided he would promise to make no attempt to seize him. The wily mayor promised, and a clearing in a nearby woods was designated as the place for the meeting. Augusta's deacon, Jacob Bilek, warned Augusta against trusting Schoeneich. "To prove that he lies," said Bilek, "I will go first to the clearing."

Bilek's suspicions were well grounded. No sooner had he stepped into the clearing than he was pounced on by three men. Discovering that they had seized the wrong man, they tied him to a tree and returned to wait for Augusta. Soon he came. That he was more suspicious than he pretended to be was evident from the fact that he was dressed as a woodcutter and carried an axe. The men seized him, looked at one another, and let the protesting woodcutter go. When he started to leave, they seized him again. Then, sure that this could not be Augusta, they released him once more. As he was leaving the clearing, the woodcutter pulled a handkerchief from a pocket. With a cry of anger the three men jumped upon Augusta. Handkerchiefs were never used by woodcutters or peasants in those days. This man was Bishop John Augusta.

"They Are Praying"

Soon faithful Bilek was in prison in a dungeon under the royal castle in Prague. John Augusta had been thrown into a cell in the White Tower. The devilish tortures intended to convert heretics to the faith of the "Mother Church" were applied to Augusta. He was smeared with pitch and the pitch was set on fire. Then the flaming blanket was peeled off of his body with iron tongs. An effort was made to squeeze a confession of heresy out of him by placing him upon the floor and piling huge stones upon his body. A hook was thrust through his flesh and he was hung up to think things over. For two days the inhuman treatments continued. When his torturers asked him what his "friends" were doing for him he replied, "They are praying to God." Bilek was tortured in similar fashion. King Ferdinand sent a message to his men, suggesting new tortures which might be used against the stubborn heretics.

The days of torture ended at last, and Augusta and Bilek were thrown into the prison in the lonely castle on Puerglitz. For sixteen years (1548-64) the martyrs lay in separate cells in a basement dungeon. The cells were lighted by tiny windows four inches square. They had nothing to read, nor would they have been able to read in the semi-darkness. No visitors were permitted.

After several years Augusta's jailors were changed, and a new group of men were given charge of the prisoners. One of the new guards turned out to be a man who had grown up in Augusta's village. He was considered a drunken rascal, worthy of no better work than guarding heretics, but he knew well enough that Augusta was guilty of no crimes. At great risk to himself he brought the bishop paper and pen and ink and candles so that he might write letters to the Brethren. He posted the letters himself and carried replies back to Augusta.

As the years passed and there seemed to be no possibility that Augusta would be released, the Brethren decided in their synods that additional bishops should be elected. To this proposal Augusta objected vigorously. He was determined not to be displaced. The man who as a youth had insisted that older men should step aside and permit the younger men who were up to date take over, now thundered from prison against younger men whom he suspected of wanting to replace him. For many years the Brethren postponed the election of additional bishops since no one wished to hurt Augusta's feelings. But at last, in 1553, it became clear that unless new bishops were chosen the episcopacy would soon come to an end in the church. So the synod selected John Czerny and Matthias Cerwenka to be bishops. Nothing was said to Augusta about what had been done. Six years passed before he learned what had taken place. Then he wrote an angry letter to the Brethren declaring that the action of synod in electing new bishops was null and void. For some years relations between Augusta and the Brethren were strained. But at long last King Ferdinand fell seriously ill. As if to prove that even a wicked man's conscience can trouble him when he looks into the face of death, he sent word that Augusta should be released from prison. In 1564 John Augusta came out into the sunshine. Immediately he and Bilek made their way to the headquarters of the Brethren. There they were received with kindness. Once more Augusta was made the chief bishop of the Brethren, and he in turn acknowledged the authority of the bishops who had been properly chosen while he was in prison. Near the end of his life (he died in 1572) Augusta wrote a hymn one stanza of which freely translated into English voices a prayer for the liberty which had been so long denied him:

Preserve for ever our sacred liberty,
As conscience prompts us, to meet and worship thee,
To thank and praise thee for thy word of grace.

Chapter 4

Darkness and Dawn

"The Happy Time Has Come"

On October 12, 1575, Emperor Maximilian II died in his castle at Regensburg, Bohemia. Shortly before his death he is said to have whispered to his friends, "The happy time has come."

Certainly for the Brethren, at least, a few years of happiness had begun. Shortly before his death the emperor had refused to recognize the Brethren's Church publicly, but he had called a large group of Lutherans and Brethren to his castle and promised them "the free exercise of their religion." His promise, he said, would be as good as a written edict.

A time of prosperity now began for the Brethren. Even though the new emperor, Rudolph II, was a Catholic and under the influence of the Jesuits, who were bitter enemies of all Protestants, the Brethren "came out into the open" throughout the land. Seventeen of the most powerful barons in the kingdom and 140 knights proclaimed themselves members of the Brethren's Church. With such support, thousands of people crowded into the Brethren's churches, and the Lord High Chamberlain of Bohemia complained that two-thirds of the people of the kingdom had gone over to the Brethren.

In dozens of towns and cities throughout the kingdom the Brethren established schools. They set up printing presses to publish Bibles and hymnbooks, school books and catechisms. Their most famous publication was the Kralitz Bible. For fourteen years (1578-1593) their best scholars patiently worked at translating the Bible from the Greek and Latin into Bohemian. Baron John von Zerotin paid the cost of the first edition. This translation standardized the Czech language much as Luther's translation did for German and the King James did for English. In order to make it possible for the common people to have copies, the Brethren published a cheap edition in plain binding. One edition after another of their hymnal came from the presses, and with the Bible and the hymnbook in the language of the people, they were able to show clearly just what the Bible really taught and to sing that faith in their churches.

"Meet Here At Six"

Although Protestantism had now become so strong that in some parts of Bohemia nine-tenths of the people were either Lutheran, Reformed, or Brethren, the Jesuits did not waver in their determination to crush and destroy Protestantism. In 1602 they persuaded Emperor Rudolph to revive the Edict of St. James. This edict, which had been issued nearly a hundred years before, prohibited meetings of the Brethren, ordered their books burned and their ministers imprisoned. Rudolph now began to enforce this ancient edict by sending a group of soldiers to Jungbunzlau to seize the church and school buildings the Brethren had in that city.

This was more than Wenzel Von Budowa proposed to endure. Budowa was a nobleman, one of the most powerful in the land. For many years he had been a faithful member of the Brethren's Church, and, having served his country as an ambassador to Constantinople, he was widely known and respected throughout the kingdom. When the emperor began seizing Protestant property, Budowa stood up in the Bohemian Diet (law-making body) and announced that if the emperor desired the obedience of his people he ought to obey the law himself. The law of the land, said Budowa, is not this ancient Edict of St. James but the Confession of 1575, which promised religious liberty to all citizens of Bohemia. Emperor Rudolph had been afraid to come to this meeting of the Diet, and he was too much of a coward now to reply, so in his anger he merely ordered all the members of the Diet to go home forthwith. For several years the Catholics made no open attacks upon the Protestants.

In 1609 the Diet was summoned again. When the Diet convened, Budowa called a meeting of all the Protestant members and the group adopted a resolution demanding that the Confession, which guaranteed religious liberty, be inserted in the statutes of the kingdom. This resolution they presented to the emperor. Five times the Protestants demanded an answer.

Then the emperor attempted to dissolve the Diet. As the members rose in confusion, Budowa placed himself at the door of the great hall and shouted loudly, "Let all who remember the courage of our fathers meet here tomorrow morning at six!"

At the appointed time the Protestants held their meeting. Word was sent to the emperor that the Protestants would fight, if necessary, for their liberty. As if to show that this was not an empty threat, petitions for help were sent to the Elector of Saxony, the Duke of Brunswick and other Protestant rulers. The nobles and knights met in the courtyard of the castle and swore with uplifted hands to be true to each other and to win the victory no matter what it might cost. Still the emperor refused to yield. "It is time to take to arms!" cried Count Thurn. At once messengers were sent throughout the kingdom to call the Protestants to battle. Citizens of Prague began to organize themselves into the first division. Finally, Emperor Rudolph gave in and signed a "Letter of Majesty" granting full religious liberty to Protestants throughout the land. To the Protestants it seemed as if the happy time had really come. In their joy, they lost sight of the fact that political solutions are never permanent, and in ten years they again faced harsh persecutions and the Day of Blood.

The Day of Blood

For a few years peace reigned in Bohemia. The Confession was faithfully observed, and Protestants and Catholics lived together as friends. Then in 1612 Emperor Rudolph died. Shortly before his death he reproached himself for having yielded to the Protestants. In fact, he went so far as to encourage Catholic landowners to insist that the Confession did not apply to persons living on their lands. Gradually serious trouble broke out in various places. Appeals to the new king produced no results. Having no children, he was busy working on a scheme to have Ferdinand, archduke of Styria, and a fanatical Catholic, succeed him. Without any consideration of the fact that Bohemia was a Protestant country, he worked out the details and then calmly announced that he had "adopted" Ferdinand as his son and, therefore, as his successor.

Ferdinand soon began to take over more and more of the duties of his aging "father." How Ferdinand felt about Protestants was apparent from the fact that when he was told that nine-tenths of the Bohemians were Protestants he replied, "Better a desert than a country full of heretics." When the king died in 1619 and Ferdinand came into full authority, it was clear that bitter days were just ahead. Although Ferdinand promised to preserve peace, most Bohemians distrusted him completely. A number of open clashes soon took place. What is called the Thirty Years War (1618-48) was beginning.

On November 8, 1620, Ferdinand and the allies he had quickly gathered fell upon the Protestants at White Mountain. No Ziska was on hand to lead them.

Frederick of the Palatinate, who had been elected king of Bohemia by the Diet, failed completely to understand the great danger threatening Protestantism. When the battle began he was not even at the scene to lead his outnumbered followers. In one terrible hour the Protestant forces were cut to pieces. When Frederick heard the news he fled for his life and did not stop running until he reached Holland. There he spent the remainder of his life in retirement.

In the very year in which the Pilgrims landed in America in search of religious liberty, the little kingdom of Bohemia witnessed the death of such liberty. Now it remained only to see what vengeance the arrogant conquerors would take.

On February 20, 1621, the Protestant nobles were ordered to meet to hear a message from the emperor. Even Count Tilly, who had become a leader of the Catholic forces, sent them a secret message urging them to flee for their lives. But because they still believed a gentleman's word, they went to the appointed place. Forty-three of them were seized and tried; forty-three were pronounced guilty. Sixteen were flogged, imprisoned and ordered sent into exile. Twenty-seven were condemned to death, fifteen of whom were members of the Brethren's Church.

June 21, 1621 has come to be known in Bohemian history as the Day of Blood. One by one the noblemen were led to the platform erected in the marketplace in Prague. First to be beheaded was Count Schlick. As he walked to the place of execution two Jesuits smiled upon him. "My Lord Count," said one, "there is still time to recant." "Let me go in peace!" cried the Count. Before he placed his head upon the block he stood erect for one last prayer: "O Christ, Thou Son of Righteousness, grant that I may, through the shadow of death, come to thy light."

Next came Budowa, the brave nobleman who had fought so hard for freedom. He was now seventy-four years of age. Even his so-called trial had not dimmed his courage. He had told the judges, "You have long thirsted for our blood. Now you will get it; but you may be sure that the shedding of our innocent blood will be followed by God's judgments, for we suffer for his cause." As he walked to the block, he stroked his silver hair and shouted. "Old grey head of mine, thou art highly honored, for thou wilt wear a martyr's crown!"

One after another they died, and the six attendants in their black robes removed their bodies. Seated under a canopy the judges watched in silence. The drums rolled and the trumpets announced the coming of each new victim. Out in the square armed guards restrained the people. All day long the sun looked down upon the terrible scene. It was only five in the morning when Count Schlick went to his death; it was ten o'clock at night before the Day of Blood was over.

The Day of Blood was the signal for a time of wild anger against Protestantism. Churches were desecrated and burned. The grave of Ziska was opened and his bones destroyed. Bohemian Bibles were seized and burned. Thousands of Protestants fled into Poland; other thousands escaped to adjoining countries. So great was the exodus that within a few years the population of Bohemia decreased from three million to less than eight hundred thousand. Ferdinand cleared his kingdom of heretics and got his desert.

The little kingdom of Bohemia never recovered from this blow. Her king had been emperor of the whole Roman Empire; her University of Prague had been the greatest in Europe; her citizens, thanks to the schools and printing presses of the Brethren, had been the best educated in Europe. Impartial historians can do no less than record this greatest achievement of the Jesuits: the deliberate and cruel destruction of a nation which, but for their vicious policies, might have remained as a great and free member of the European family of nations.

Something to Look At

During the unhappy days preceding the Day of Blood an orphan was growing up in the neighboring kingdom of Moravia. John Amos Comenius was born on March 28, 1592. His parents, who were members of the Brethren's Church, died when John was a small boy and relatives sent him to a Brethren's school. When he announced that he desired to become a minister, he was sent to a theological institute and later to the University of Heidelberg. In 1616 he was appointed headmaster of a Brethren's high school at Fulneck in Moravia.

The importance of Comenius in the educational world is apparent from the fact that his name is among those engraved upon the library of Congress. It appears also upon the main building of Teachers' College at Columbia University. We like to remember also that when Harvard University was being established, Governor John Winthrop invited Comenius to come to America to become its president.

One may sum up the achievements of Comenius by saying that it was he who first introduced pictures into school books. His *Orbis Pictus*, for instance, consisted of pictures illustrating various trades. One page of the book had a picture of a shoemaker at his work. Every object in the picture was numbered. Beneath the picture were two columns, Latin on the right, the child's own language on the left.

With this kind of book children easily learned not only words, but their meanings as well. Comenius' books were translated into many languages and his theories of teaching found wide acceptance. One of his principles was "The teacher must be kind and fatherly, must distribute praise and reward, and must always, where it is possible, give the children something to look at." When we think of what most schools were like in the days of Comenius, we see what great new ideas a simple statement like this contained. Comenius believed that children belonged to God and that it was a teacher's privilege to help them grow up to be Christians.

The Wandering Bishop

When the Thirty Years War broke out in 1618, Comenius was happy in his position at the school in Fulneck. In 1620 Ferdinand's troops appeared in the peaceful little town. Soldiers ran from house to house, pillaging and burning. The books of Comenius were seized, taken to the village square, and burned. For a few months Comenius and his family managed to hide, then they were forced to flee to the estate of a wealthy nobleman, Baron Von Zerotin. During the flight, his wife and one of his children died. At thirty years of age the young teacher had lost both his family and his possessions. In his sorrow he wrote a wonderful little book called *The Labyrinth of the World*. It was like *Pilgrim's Progress* (which had not yet been written) and told the story of a pilgrim wandering through the world, mistreated and abused by Mr. Knowlittle, Mr. Lovestrife, Mr. Nogod, and others. At last the pilgrim finds happiness in the church in which good men and women endeavor to follow Christ.

When it seemed as if there would be no letup in the persecution of the Protestants, Comenius and a few friends made a secret trip to Poland to see whether they could find a place of refuge among Brethren who had fled from Bohemia years before. They were successful in their mission, and in January 1628 Comenius led a little band of refugees across the Giant Mountains into Poland. When they reached the boundary of their land, the group paused to look for the last time upon their homeland. Comenius lifted his hands in prayer, asking God to prevent his truth from being blotted out in old Bohemia. "Preserve there," he prayed, "a hidden seed to glorify thy Name."

In Poland the Brethren found a hearty welcome. A small city named Lissa became their headquarters. In 1632 Comenius and three other ministers were consecrated bishops. In 1636 Comenius was made head of the college the Brethren established in Lissa. For about twenty years the Brethren had another "happy time" in their new home.

Then in 1652 the Catholic Bishop of Posen announced that the building used by the Brethren in that city had originally been a Catholic church. The Catholics, he said, would therefore repossess it. The Brethren insisted that the building had never belonged to the Catholics; but when the case was tried, they lost the building. Much more serious trials were just ahead. In 1655 King Charles of Sweden invaded Poland. Charles was a Protestant, and it is plain that most of the Protestants in Poland hoped he would conquer the country (some of them did more than merely hope). But at last Charles was driven out, and the enemies of Protestantism had the excuse for which they had been waiting. Lissa was plundered and burned to the ground. The Brethren were beaten and prosecuted. Once more Comenius fled for his life. Once more his books and his possessions were destroyed (except for a few manuscripts he managed to bury). For forty years he had been working on a Latin-Bohemian dictionary. The manuscript of that work the soldiers burned along with everything else they could lay their hands upon. "The loss of this work," Comenius said later, "I shall cease to lament only when I die." For a time

Comenius lived in hiding. Then came a warm invitation from Lawrence de Geer, a prominent citizen of Amsterdam, promising a safe refuge. This invitation Comenius was happy to accept.

Will the Brethren's Church Die?

Throughout the years of bitter persecution Comenius seems to have clung to one hope: "Some day, with God's help, our church will live again in a happier land." Although he was now compelled to live in Holland, he did everything he could to help his brethren. In 1657 he sent representatives to England to ask English Christians for help. The name of Comenius was well known in England, and his appeal produced amazing results. English Protestants sent Comenius no less than $30,000. With this money Bohemian and Polish Bibles were published and in places where groups of Brethren could find a refuge they were helped to rebuild their churches. In 1660 Comenius published the *Ratio Disciplinae*, a Latin book containing a history of the Brethren and an explanation of their teachings. This book he dedicated to the Church of England, saying that he felt his Brethren's Church was dying and urging the English church to love and care for his church. Comenius had not entirely given up hope, as it is apparent from the fact that in this same dedication he asserted, "If there is no help from man, there will only be help from God." In the spirit of this assertion he and the only other remaining bishop of the Brethren agreed that additional bishops should be chosen *in spem contra spem* (hoping even where there seems to be no hope). In 1662 two bishops were chosen. One of them was Peter Jablonsky, Comenius's son-in-law.

Comenius died in Amsterdam in 1670, at the age of seventy-eight. "My whole life," he wrote, "is merely the visit of a guest. I have no fatherland." But the wandering bishop's real fatherland was the home above of which he had written in his *Labyrinth*, and today this great "man without a country" is honored in all countries everywhere.

Fifty Years of Waiting

Fifty years passed before the hopes of Comenius could be realized. During these years some of the Brethren went back to Poland and rebuilt the town of Lissa. But in 1707 the town was sacked and burned again, this time by a Russian army. Many of the Brethren now lost heart completely. Some of them joined the Reformed Church, which had now been established in Poland. A few tiny congregations continued to hold out in spite of everything. Back in Bohemia and Moravia little groups of Brethren likewise held together. They could hold no public services. On nights when snow was falling they often dared to walk single file out of a village into the woods. The last man in line carefully covered the tell-tale footprints with a branch, and the snow would soon hide all traces of their little journey. In the heart of the woods they would huddle closely together in a solid circle, and by the light of a tiny fire their leader would read from the Bohemian Bible. Now and then a minister from the Brethren's Church in Skalic, Hungary, would manage to slip into Bohemia or Moravia and visit these little groups and celebrate the holy communion with them. Now and then help and encouragement would come from Prussia, where the Brethren's Bishop Jablonsky (son of the bishop referred to above) was court preacher. He was able, because of his friendship with Frederick I of Prussia, to help them in many ways.

Jesuit missionaries went up and down the little kingdoms of Bohemia and Moravia. In order to aid them in finding Protestants, they introduced the custom of having priests issue certificates to everyone who attended confession. To be unable to produce such a certificate upon demand meant that one was a Protestant. Imprisonment was a mild punishment for so serious an offense.

"The Time Is Near"

But, *in spem contra spem*, as Comenius would have put it, the faith lived on. In 1707—the very year in which the burning of Lissa seemed to quench all hope for the Brethren in Poland—an old man, whose name was George Jaeschke, lay dying in his home at Sehlen, Moravia. Gathering his children around him he urged them to hold fast to their faith in Christ. "It may seem as though the final days of the Brethren's Church have come," he said. "But, my dear children, you will see a great deliverance. I do not know whether it will come to pass here in Moravia, or whether you will have to go out of this Babylon, but I do know that it will come before very long. I am inclined to believe that a journey will take place, and that a refuge will be offered in a country where you will be able, without fear, to serve the Lord according to his holy Word. When that time comes, be ready for it; give diligence that you may not be the last or remain behind."

At ten o'clock on the evening of May 27, 1722, a little band of men and women met in Jacob Neisser's home, in the very town in which father Jaeschke had died. They prayed together, said farewell to their friends, opened the door softly, and went out, one by one, into the night. Christian David was their leader and they were beginning a journey to Saxony, where a kind-hearted count had offered them a place of refuge. One of the group was Michael, a son of George Jaeschke. Now that the time of deliverance had come, he was ready for it. His father's dream was about to be realized. In a new land the Brethren's Church was to rise from the ashes of destruction. "The hidden seed" for which Comenius had prayed nearly a century before was about to spring into life and bear fruit.

Chapter 5

The Golden Decade

In the reviving of the Brethren's Church two men were to play an important part. One was a poor carpenter; the other was a wealthy nobleman. Strange as it may seem, neither man had grown up in the church he was destined to bless so richly.

Looking for the Light

The older of the two men was Christian David, born in Moravia on New Year's Eve, 1690. His parents were Catholic, and he was taught, as he himself said in later years, to hate Protestants with a hatred "hot as a baking oven." In spite of this teaching, however, the growing boy was greatly impressed by the courage of Protestants in his town who were willing to suffer for their faith. "Why do they hold on to this faith," he asked himself, "when it brings them nothing but trouble?" He decided that he would try to find out, so he went to a Protestant family and asked them to tell him about their religion. They told him plainly that the pope was really the Anti-Christ (that is, the great enemy of Christ who is mentioned in the Bible), that it was wrong to pray to saints, and that only Jesus could forgive sins. Worried by what he had done, the lad consulted Catholic friends who told him just as emphatically that Protestants were "children of the Devil." Poor Christian David was more confused than ever.

The Bible promises that anyone who sincerely desires to know the truth will be able to find it. So it was with Christian David. In 1710 he succeeded in obtaining a Bible. Day by day he studied it and carefully copied verses to memorize. Little by little the blessed truths of the Scriptures began to clear away the fog in his mind. He began to associate more and more with Protestant neighbors. Some of them were suspicious of him and gave him little help; others did what they could to help him find the truth he was seeking.

How Christian David Found the Truth

In 1717, while looking for work, Christian David came to the town of Goerlitz in Silesia. There he became seriously ill and for twenty weeks he was flat upon his back. Day after day a kindly Lutheran pastor, John Schwedler, visited him, cared for him, let him talk out all his doubts and questions, and told him, in turn, by deeds as well as by words, of the Savior of who all believe. During the long weeks of illness the seeker found the truth and was glad.

As soon as he was well, a great desire to tell others about the joy he had found took hold upon him. "Whom shall I tell?" he asked himself. The answer seemed to be: "The persecuted people among whom I grew up!"

Before long the young man, at great risk to himself, began making secret trips back to Moravia. Visiting Protestant communities, he preached the faith which had changed his own life. In the hearts of persecuted members of the Brethren's Church these visits of their countryman stirred up new hope and courage. Perhaps, they said to themselves, Christian David may be able to find a place of refuge for us among his good friends in Silesia or elsewhere. When they asked him about this, Christian David promised to do what he could.

Several years passed before the young man's efforts bore fruit. Wherever it was safe for him to do so, he spoke about the persecuted Protestants in Moravia. Early in the spring of 1722 Count Nicholas Louis von Zinzendorf heard about him and asked to see him. Eagerly Christian David poured out his story. The count said that he would use his influence to try to find a place for these people. If any of them cared to come at once, they might settle temporarily on his own estate. "I will give them land to build on," he put it, "and Christ will give them the rest."

Christian David hurried back to Moravia. Bursting into the home of the Neissers he announced that a Saxon nobleman named Zinzendorf had promised a place of refuge for persecuted Protestants. "This is God's doing," said Augustine and Jacob Neisser. At ten o'clock on the evening of May 27, 1722, the two brothers with their wives and children and two friends, ten in all, stepped out of the Neisser home into the night. Quietly they walked down the dear street they were to see no more and out of the town, to follow Christian David to their land of promise.

The Young Count

Who was this Count Zinzendorf whose kind promise led to things of which he had never dreamed?

He was born in Dresden, capital of the kingdom of Saxony, in 1700. His grandfather had left his native Austria for the sake of his faith and now the family had become wealthy and prominent in Saxony. He was still a tiny baby when his father died. When he was four years old, his mother married again and moved to Berlin. From that time on little Louis lived with his grandmother in the castle at Hennersdorf.

After having been taught at home for several years the young count was sent to Francke's school at Halle. Unfortunately, Comenius's principle, "The teacher must be kind and fatherly," had not yet been heard of at Halle. The public whipping of pupils was almost an everyday event. Sometimes such exhibitions were even advertised in advance upon the bulletin board. More than once appeared the notice: "Next week the count is to have the rod." Zinzendorf's fellow students apparently were not any kinder to him than the masters; to them he was a snob who had money to spend. How to get some of that money for themselves was the only thing about him which was of interest to many of the other boys.

It took the unhappy count, who was only ten years old when he arrived, several years to learn how to defend himself. But the bitter experiences he suffered were not without results. They taught him how to endure unjust abuse; they taught him to "take it to the Lord in prayer." Earnestly he prayed that he might grow up to be a good man. After a while it occurred to him that he need not wait until he was grown to be a Christian. When he was fifteen, he and another young count, Frederick de Watteville, and a few companions, organized a society which they named "The Order of the Grain of Mustard Seed." Members of the group took a pledge of loyalty to Christ and promised to speak no slander, honor a promise made, live clean lives. (In later years this society became famous. Governor Oglethorpe of Georgia, Archbishop Potter of Canterbury, and even the Catholic Cardinal Noailles wore the gold ring of the order founded by a few schoolboys.)

It was while he was still in Francke's school that another great idea was planted in Zinzendorf's mind. Because he was a count he ate at the headmaster's table (perhaps this accounted for some of his troubles with fellow students), and one day the headmaster had a distinguished guest, a Danish missionary named Ziegenbalg. Young Zinzendorf was greatly touched by the stories the missionary told. He and his friend de Watteville decided that if God would show them how to do it, they would use the money they expected to have some day in sending missionaries to the heathen.

At sixteen Zinzendorf was ready for the university. His guardian had already decided that the count was to become a court official of some kind, so the boy was sent to Wittenberg to study government and law. Zinzendorf applied himself diligently to his studies, but spent his free time reading the writings of Martin Luther and talking to the professors of theology.

Upon graduation he was sent, in accordance with the custom among wealthy families of that day, on a tour. On this tour he was introduced to William of Orange and other princes and noblemen. He spent half a year in

Paris. He formed a friendship with Cardinal Noailles and had long talks with him about the differences between the Catholics and the Protestants. But something which happened to him in the art gallery at Duesseldorf made the greatest impression of all.

While wandering among the pictures in the gallery the young count came suddenly upon a picture of Christ with the crown of thorns. Beneath the picture was the Latin question: "Hoc tibi feci, quid mihi fecisti?" Quickly Zinzendorf translated it: "I have done this for you; what have you done for me?" The tears came to his eyes. "I have loved him for a long time," he said to himself, "but I have never actually done anything for him. From now on I will do whatever he leads me to do!"

Had he been able to follow his own desires, he would have entered the ministry, but even his pious grandmother insisted that such a calling was beneath a nobleman, so he became a counselor at the royal court in Dresden. But because he wanted very greatly to keep in touch with common people, he took some of the money which came to him when he came of age and bought the estate of Berthelsdorf from his grandmother so that he might be able, now and then, at least to "live among the peasants and win their souls for Christ." He was soon to have an opportunity for doing this very thing. It was in April 1722 that the estate came onto his hands. It was on June 8 of the same year that Christian David and his little band of pilgrims arrived in Berthelsdorf.

The Establishment of Herrnhut

Zinzendorf was in Dresden when the refugees arrived. His caretaker, good-hearted John Heitz, was puzzled to know what to do with the strangers, so he put them up temporarily and began to think. After a few days he decided to find a suitable spot somewhere on the estate and let the newcomers build a house for themselves. On the morning of June 17 he led them to a hill about a mile from the village. Here there was an open space where gypsies sometimes camped. There were pine and beech trees nearby. Here, he said, the settlers might build themselves a house.

It was a hard moment for the little group. Augustine Neisser's wife began to cry. "Where shall we find bread in this wilderness?" she asked. Christian David, however, seized an axe and began to cut down the nearest tree, shouting, as the chips flew, "Yea, the sparrow hath found her a house, and the swallow a nest for herself, where she may lay her young, even thine altars, O Lord of hosts, my King and my God" (Psalm 84:3).

Throughout the summer the settlers worked on their house. Lady Gersdorf sent them a cow so that they might have milk for their children. Had it not been for her kindness and the friendly interest of the caretaker, they would probably have starved to death. John Heitz became more and more interested in the refugees. Whenever he could spare a bit of time from his many duties he came up the hill and helped the builders. He wrote to Zinzendorf about the new "town" which was being built, and it was he who named the place Herrnhut, The Lord's Watch (that is, the place God will guard).

Home for Christmas

Early in the fall the new house was completed. As yet the new settlers had not even seen their landlord. They rejoiced, however, when they heard that he had married countess Erdmuth Dorothea Reuss, and they were happy to hear good reports of her and her family. During November they heard that the count and his bride were planning to come home for Christmas.

It was on the evening of December 2 that the coach containing the count and the countess came along the road leading to Hennersdorf. Soon after the count had tried to show his wife as best he could in the darkness where his lands began, he noticed a strange light shining through the trees. In reply to his question the coachman said, "That is where the exiles from Moravia live."

Zinzendorf immediately directed the coachman to stop at the house. He knocked at the door and when it was opened, he introduced himself. He was warmly welcomed by the settlers; he in turn assured them that they were welcome on his land. Then kneeling down upon the rough floor, he asked God to bless these people who had forsaken home and country for the gospel of Christ.

Now that they felt safe and happy in their new home the settlers sent a messenger back to their relatives in Moravia. The messenger found that in their anger over the secret departure of the first group, authorities had imprisoned a number of the relatives of the emigrants. But even jailors often showed their sympathy by forgetting to lock the gates at night. Soon a new group of eighteen persons was on its way to Herrnhut.

Early in 1723 Zinzendorf asked Christian David and a group of the men in the little settlement if they would be willing to work on the new manor house he planned to erect in the village. They were very happy for this means of supporting themselves and went to work with a will.

One day in December Christian David suddenly laid down his tools and announced, "I am going back to Moravia to bring more of the Brethren to this happy place." Off he went, back to the villages from which the first settlers had come. Secretly he went from house to house, telling everyone of the liberty and freedom to be found in Herrnhut.

In the village of Zauchtenthal he met five young men who had banded themselves together for the express purpose of keeping the old Brethren's Church alive. As they listened to Christian David's glowing account of Herrnhut, they were impressed but not entirely convinced. "Would it not be better," they asked, "for us to go to Poland? Our church was so well established there; surely there are still Brethren there in spite of everything that has happened." Christian David had no knowledge of conditions in Poland, but what he knew about Herrnhut he knew with all his heart, and when he continued urging them, the five young men finally said, "Well, we'll stop at Herrnhut on our way to Poland."

It was May 12, 1724, when the five young men arrived in Herrnhut. Three of them bore the name David Nitschmann; the other two were Melchior Zeisberger and John Toeltschig. They had expected to find a town; instead they found three houses. As they stood in the clearing not knowing quite what to think, one of the David Nitschmanns said, "Well, if three houses make a city, there are worse places than Herrnhut!" After a while Count Zinzendorf arrived with the countess, and the settlers began assembling for a service. It appeared that they were about to lay the cornerstone of a school building. Count de Watteville offered a prayer which touched the hearts of the young men. Then he took off his jewelry and placed it in the cornerstone. Count Zinzendorf spoke of the city of God which was being erected in the woods. The five young men looked at one another. "Let's stay right here," they said, "and go to work."

During the next few years a steady stream of emigrants came from Moravia. Ten times Christian David journeyed back home to lead groups of settlers to the new town. The three houses really grew into a small city. Many of the new arrivals had thrilling tales to tell of the ways in which sympathetic Catholic friends had helped them escape. The father of one of the five young men had been thrown into prison in the tower of a castle. One night he saw a rope hanging in front of his window and with its help he slid to the ground and started for Herrnhut. David Nitschmann, "the wheelwright," (so called to distinguish him from the other David Nitschmanns) and David Schneider had been put into prison and chained to the wall. One night they discovered that their chains had not been fastened to the wall. When they investigated further they found that the prison door was unlocked. In one town Officer David Hickel was ordered on several occasions to pursue fleeing Protestants. Every time he saw them ahead of him in the woods he warned them by singing loudly. The result was that he never quite caught them. At last the angry authorities guessed the truth and put Hickel into prison, ordering the jailor to starve him for three days. After he had been in prison for some time, the noticed one day that both his guards had their backs turned toward him. When he tried the handle of the door he found the bolt was not in place. Quickly he walked out, bade his friends a hasty farewell, and set out on the ten days' journey to Herrnhut.

Chickens and Sparrows

In the Old Testament we read that when Saul was seeking to kill David, David's friends rallied around him at the cave of Adullam. Soon he had quite an army. Unfortunately, as soon as news of what was taking place got around, "everyone that was in distress, and everyone that was in debt, and everyone that was discontented" (1 Samuel 22:2) came too, and tried to "join up."

That was about what happened during the early days of Herrnhut. As soon as people heard that persecuted Protestants were being allowed to settle on Zinzendorf's estate, all kinds of unhappy people, some of whom had never been persecuted at all, came too. "When one feeds the chickens," an English historian put it, "the sparrows come too."

Within five years Herrnhut was a very unhappy town. Some of the 300 inhabitants said, "This is a Moravian town. God brought us here so that we might reestablish our church." Others asked, "Who are these Moravians anyway? Zinzendorf is a Lutheran, therefore this is a Lutheran town." To make matters worse, a man named John Krueger, who was angry at the Lutherans because they had expelled him for teaching false doctrines and who had never heard of the Moravians, arrived in Herrnhut. He promptly took a great dislike to Zinzendorf and marched around the little town telling everybody that the count was none other than "the Beast" mentioned in the book of Revelation! Unfortunately some folks listened to Krueger. Even Christian David went so far as to move out of the village and build a cabin for himself in the woods. Although poor Krueger soon had to be taken to an insane asylum, the seeds he had sown continued to grow. Some of the settlers refused to go to the "wicked " parish church. For a time it seemed as if the community might destroy itself.

Zinzendorf was determined that this should not happen, so he took a leave of absence from his court duties and came back to Herrnhut. After visiting among his settlers for a while, he called a mass meeting for May 12, 1727. For three hours he spoke to the people, reminding them in kindly but firm tones that they were living on his land. He did not intend, he said, to permit quarreling to break up the settlement. He had therefore, he added, drawn up a set of rules and would insist that everybody sign them.

The effect of this meeting was good. Most of the settlers shook hands with one another. Shortly after the meeting Christian David moved back into the village. Zinzendorf now felt sure the situation was not hopeless. Throughout the summer of 1727 he went from house to house, praying for and with each family. He learned at first hand the religious views of the people and tried to show them how important it was that all who professed to love the Savior should love one another also.

Gradually the clouds of bitterness began to blow away. On July 2 more than a thousand people from Herrnhut, Berthelsdorf, and surrounding communities gathered at the Lutheran church. Pastor Schwedler preached to those in the building while Pastor Rothe preached to the overflow in the churchyard.

The Influence of a Book

A few days later a strange thing happened. Zinzendorf had gone to the library at Zittau. There he came suddenly upon a copy of Comenius's *Ratio Disciplinae*. Because he had heard many of his settlers refer to Comenius, he sat down and began to read the book. The more he read, the better he began to understand the feeling of the group which kept saying, "God has brought us here so that he might restore our church." He was startled to discover that the faith of Comenius and his Brethren's Church was very close to what he himself believed. The words, "If there is no help from man, there will be help from God," touched him deeply.

"I could not read the lamentations of old Comenius," he said later, "without resolving then and there: I, as far as I can, will help to bring about this renewal. Though I have to sacrifice my earthly possessions, my honor and my life, I will do my utmost to see to it that this little flock of the Lord shall be preserved for him, until he come."

Hurrying back to Herrnhut, Zinzendorf spoke to many of the original settlers about his discovery. With new zeal they promised one another to work and pray for the accomplishment of what God must have had in mind when the town was established.

On August 13 came the greatest blessing of all. Pastor Rothe had invited the people of Herrnhut to join in a celebration of the holy communion at the Berthelsdorf church. As the citizens of the little town walked down the hill to the church, "those who had been estranged one from the other," an old record puts it, "cordially embraced one another."

The service opened with the hymn, "Unbind Me, O My God, From All My Bonds and Fetters." Two girls who had completed their instruction were confirmed. Everyone knelt in prayer as the hymn "My Soul Before Thee Prostrate Lies" was sung. By this time many of those present could not sing. The old bitterness, the hard words, and the anger were all being washed away in a flood of tears. "We learned to love," one of those present wrote later. One after another opened his heart in confession and prayer, and the Lord heard and answered. James Montgomery's poem puts it this way:

> He found them in the House of Prayer
> With one accord assembled,
> And so revealed his presence there;
> They wept for joy and trembled;
> One cup they drank, one bread they broke,
> One baptism shared, one language spoke,
> Forgiving and forgiven.

After the service closed members of the congregation stood around outside talking about the blessing they had received and renewing broken friendships. Zinzendorf suddenly had an inspiration. He sent up to the manor house and had food sent to six or seven homes in the community. In these homes members of the congregation gathered and had simple meals together. Zinzendorf was reminded of the way in which the early Christians often ate together as an expression of their love for one another. Soon it became customary to have, every now and then, what we now call a lovefeast—a simple meal served in the church as an expression of mutual love. Early Moravians often gave lovefeasts on their birthdays. There were farewell lovefeasts for departing missionaries, lovefeasts for the married people, the young men, the young women and the children.

Shortly after the August 13 communion service the Brethren began the "Hourly Intercession." So that some members of their church would *always* be praying they worked out a schedule whereby one man and one woman were assigned to every hour of the day and night. For more than one hundred years this plan was carried out without a break. It was, as someone has said, "the longest prayer meeting on record."

While their parents were having these blessed experiences the children were deeply affected also. Zinzendorf was very fond of children. "Children are little kings," he once said, "their baptism is their anointing." During the summer of 1727 a theological student named Krumpe was appointed to be the pastor of the children. Pastor Krumpe was a good man and worked faithfully with the boys and girls. Throughout the summer he held special meetings for the children. An eleven-year-old girl, Susanna Kuehnel, took a leading part in what is often called the Children's Revival, and it is important to remember that many of the missionaries and leaders of the Moravian Church in later years came from the ranks of those who had first learned to love Jesus during the summer of 1727.

Life in Herrnhut

As the town of Herrnhut grew, Zinzendorf felt it necessary to set up a simple government for the community. Twelve men were appointed elders who served also as a kind of town council. They levied the necessary taxes, kept the streets in order, supervised the digging of wells, approved (or disapproved) of plans for houses. The elders had other powers also: no man could marry without proving that he could support a wife; after he was married the elders could punish him if he mistreated his wife; they could also punish the wife if she was a trouble-maker.

In the little town the day began at 5 a.m., when citizens were awakened by the town crier shouting:

The clock is at five! Five virgins will be lost

And five will be welcomed at the marriage!

As quickly as possible everyone gathered in the Hall for morning prayers. At six o'clock the crier called once more:

The clock is at six! Now I give up watching;

Now each of you must be his own watchman!

With that cry the day's work began, and the crier went home to bed. At eight in the evening he began his work again with the cry:

The clock is at eight! Herrnhut, remember
How Noah was preserved, eight with himself!

At nine came the Singstunde (song service), and soon after that everyone was glad to go to bed!

It was during these early days in Herrnhut that the Daily Text Book had its origin. It became customary for the count, at the evening song service, to give the people a verse of Scripture and a hymn verse. Next morning the elders took this text and hymn verse to every home in the village as a motto for the day. In 1728 a large number of suitable texts and hymn verses were selected and placed in a box. From that time on, one card was drawn every evening. In 1730 the texts and verses for a whole year were printed in advance, so the Daily Text Book was born. This little volume of daily devotions is now printed in thirty-eight languages every year. A million and a quarter copies are sold every year in all Moravian areas throughout the world, and the circulation exceeds the membership of the Moravian Church nearly three times.

Looking for Friends

The growth of the village of Herrnhut attracted much attention throughout Saxony. Some of the attention was favorable, but much of it was not. Zinzendorf soon found himself being accused of many crimes, not the least of which was the sheltering of a group of "Moravians" who had probably left their homes for no good reason anyway. Somewhat worried about what might happen to Herrnhut, Zinzendorf determined to make as many friends for himself and the Moravians as he possibly could. He went to the university at Jena and visited with the students and professors. He so impressed the learned professor Spangenberg that he resigned his position and moved to Herrnhut. The count went to other universities, also, and sent messengers to prominent persons whose friendship he was anxious to have for himself and his people.

In 1728 three young men were sent to London to seek the friendship of Countess Schaumburg-Lippe. The three men had to earn their passage as best they could. They walked into Holland and got through a part of that country by working on boats. They slept wherever they could find shelter. One night they had to sleep under the sky on a dike. Because it was chilly they divided the night into three parts, so that each man might have a turn at sleeping between the other two. In Brielle they met a man who hailed them as "brothers" and invited them to his house. When they arrived he showed them a fine room. When they explained that they could not pay for such accommodations he turned them out into the street. Finally, hungry and nearly exhausted, they arrived in Rotterdam. A stranger approached them and asked them if they wanted to go to England. When they said, "Yes," he took them to a sea captain who offered them free passage to London. There persons who had heard of Zinzendorf entertained them. The countess was most kind to them, and listened gladly to everything they told her about their church and their faith. After several days she herself took them back to Rotterdam on a royal yacht. In a few more weeks they were back in Herrnhut. They had made firm friends for their church in both Holland and England.

Two other young Herrnhuters made a trip to Copenhagen. They too walked until they had worn out their heavy shoes. One night they had a bit of money, so they decided to sleep in a real bed for a change. But when they knocked at the door of a little inn, the innkeeper took one look at their clothing and shouted, as he slammed the door, "Beggars must go elsewhere!" When they reached their destination, Prince Charles and Princess Sophia received them graciously, even though John Nitschmann, who was not accustomed to bowing to royalty, lost his balance in executing the gesture and fell down against the woodbox, knocking it over with a great clatter! When he had recovered from his embarrassment, he told his kind hosts how he had been imprisoned for his faith back in Moravia and how he had escaped to Herrnhut. He described the little community which had been established and said that most of its members were anxious to be "true witnesses for Jesus." The prince and the princess wept as they listened to his simple story. When John and his companion started for home they knew that they were leaving behind them firm friends in the royal Danish household.

Humble men like these did not go on long hard journeys in order to see the world. They went in order to be "witnesses for Jesus," as they put it. They went out of love for their church, so that their church might have firm friends in other lands if their enemies should succeed in scattering them again.

Within a few years many of these men, and other men and women like them were to leave Herrnhut, but not in hasty flight. They were destined to go as messengers of the gospel of peace. The worldwide missionary work of the Moravian Church was about to begin.

Chapter 6

How the Moravians Became Missionaries

A King and a Slave

In 1731 Count Zinzendorf received an invitation to attend the coronation of Christian VI as king of Denmark. He called a meeting of the Herrnhut settlers, read the invitation to them, and asked if they thought he ought to go. Some of the Brethren had little use for kings, so they said, "No." The majority, however, voted "Yes." Preparations for the journey got under way at once. Strange as it may seem, when Zinzendorf returned from Copenhagen he had very little to say about the coronation; one might almost have concluded that he had never seen the new king at all. The first thing he did was to call a meeting of the settlers and tell them not of the king, but of a slave named Anthony whom he had met in Copenhagen. Anthony had been brought by his master from the West Indies. He had told Zinzendorf about his brother and sister back in the Islands and of the hard and bitter lives of the slaves who were taught nothing about God and knew only the cruel whips of their masters. The count said that he felt the words of Anthony were a call from the Lord, and he announced that he had arranged to have Anthony himself come to Herrnhut and tell his story.

Sleepless Night

That night two of the young men who had attended the meeting could not sleep; hour after hour they heard the watchman's song. When Leonard Dober arose early the next morning, he had made a great decision: the Lord was calling him to go to the West Indies as a missionary. All day long he turned the matter over in his mind. That evening he and his friend Tobias Leopold went for a walk in the woods. After a while Dober found courage enough to confide his feeling to his friend. Leopold listened in amazement, then burst out, "I could not sleep last night either. I heard the Voice in my heart, too."

On the very next day, July 25, 1731, the two friends met and carefully wrote a letter to Count Zinzendorf offering to go to the West Indies as missionaries. Their letter was a long one and it closed with the prayer: "May the Lord lead us in the right path, rough though that path may be."

Count Zinzendorf was thrilled. He read the letter to the congregation without revealing the names of the writers. Several days later Anthony arrived in Herrnhut and spoke to the congregation. "If missionaries go to the West Indies," he said, "they may find it necessary to become slaves themselves if they wish to reach the people." Slaves, he continued, were not permitted to leave their plantations after sunset. Teaching them was forbidden, nor were they permitted to attend public worship. A slave who had driven his master's carriage to church had been cruelly whipped because he had dared to peep through the doors of the church at the worshipers inside. But everything Anthony told the congregation only strengthened the desire burning in the hearts of the two young men.

"Let the Lad Go!"

The two volunteers soon discovered, however, that not everyone shared their enthusiasm. Many members of the congregation said openly that the entire plan was only a sample of the crazy ideas young folks sometimes get. For a number of months the discussion went on; then Dober wrote to the congregation once more, repeating his offer. Count Zinzendorf then said the matter should be put to the lot. The congregation gathered and a box was brought into the room. Into the box had been placed slips of paper with "yes" or "no" quotations from the Bible. After earnest prayer that God would guide the hand which drew out a slip, Leonard Dober reached into the box, opened the slip he had drawn, and read, "Let the lad go, for the Lord is with him."

Within a few weeks final plans had been completed. Dober was a potter; it was agreed therefore that David Nitschmann, a carpenter, should go with him to stay for several months and help him establish himself in the new land. On the evening of August 18, 1732, the farewell meeting was held in Herrnhut. Zinzendorf told the story of all that had happened since his visit to Copenhagen. "Then they sang," says an old record, "one after another, according to their custom in those days, their hearty good wishes in verses of hymns. . .more than a hundred verses were sung." Two days later at three o'clock in the morning Count Zinzendorf started out in his carriage with the two missionaries. Near Bautzen the three men got out of the carriage, prayed together and said farewell. Before the two missionaries started down the dusty road in the direction of Copenhagen, several hundred miles away, Zinzendorf gave them the best advice he could: "Let yourselves be guided in all things by the spirit of Jesus Christ."

When the two friends arrived in Copenhagen they discovered that the Danish West India Company would have nothing to do with taking missionaries to the West Indies. Undaunted, they appealed directly to the queen, who listened to their story with great interest. Soon the royal household was busy. The royal chamberlain, the princess and others gave them money. The court physician gave them medicines and a few medical instruments. The royal cupbearer found a ship bound for St. Thomas, in the West Indies. Her owner was very glad to take friends of the queen with him. The ship happened to be a Dutch ship. Here again the good hand of God was seen: for, as the missionaries discovered, the natives on St. Thomas spoke Dutch (because the island had once belonged to the Netherlands) and the Dutch they picked up on shipboard was a great help to them later on.

On Saturday morning, December 13, 1732, the two missionaries stood upon the deck looking at the little island of St. Thomas. They noted the yellow rocks along the shore and the whiteness of the sand and the dark redwood shingles on the roofs of the buildings in the little town of Tappus. As the ship sailed slowly into the harbor, they turned to their Daily Text Book for a word of blessing. Strange were the words of the first text for the day: "The Lord of Hosts mustereth out the host for the battle!"

The Beginnings

The first thing the new missionaries did was to hunt for Abraham and Anna, brother and sister of the slave Anthony. When they had found them, they read them the letter which Anthony had sent for them. Anthony had closed his letter with the words: "This is life eternal, that they might know Thee the only true God, and Jesus Christ whom Thou hast sent." Taking these words of Christ as a "text," the two men preached their first sermon to the group of curious slaves who had gathered around them. In spite of their halting Dutch the slaves understood at least some parts of their message, for they clapped their hands and cried for joy. For the first time in their lives the gospel had been preached directly to them.

That evening Dober and Nitschmann went to the public service held at the fort in Tappus. As they came out of the hall a slave approached them. His master, he said, would like to meet them. Soon it turned out that the master was a man named Lorenzen who had once known Zinzendorf. Now, for old times' sake, he offered the two missionaries work on a house he was building.

This kind offer they were happy to accept. As they accompanied their new friend to his plantation, they told themselves that their work was going to be easier than they had dared hope it would be.

Every evening, when their work on the house was done, the missionaries went from one plantation to another, preaching to the slaves. The slaves listened attentively, but the missionaries soon began to feel that their words were not making a very deep impression. Within a few weeks they discovered the reasons for this.

They learned that there were about 3,000 slaves on the little island and only 300 planters. They soon saw that the planters maintained their rule by cruelty and oppression. Their laws were designed to keep the slaves in such fear and terror that they would not think of rebelling. For the slightest offense a slave was cruelly whipped; for a second offense his ears were chopped off; for a third offense he was hanged. His head was then cut off and nailed up on a post along the road as a grim warning to every passer-by. Slaves were forbidden to marry. When planters discovered slaves living together as members of a family, they broke up the home by selling the husband or wife into another section of the island or to a trader from another island. The natural consequences of the white man's rule was that no slave ever quite trusted a white man. Dober and Nitschmann soon saw that their work was not going to be as easy as they had assumed it would be.

The Lone Watchman

In four months Nitschmann returned home as he had been instructed to do. The planter's house was completed, so the lonely Dober decided to try to earn a living by working at his trade. But although he searched in every corner of the island, he could find no clay suitable for making pottery. Many of the planters laughed loudly at him, and poor Dober became more and more discouraged. Then one day Governor Gardelin come to him. "I have watched you for a long time," he said. "I will give you a position as steward in my house. I offer you this because I believe you are a Christian."

Dober's worries seemed at an end. He ate at the governor's table; he even bought a new suit of clothes. But alas, he soon discovered that his influence as a missionary was at an end also. The slaves still listened to him, but they whispered to one another, "Do not trust him; he has gone over to the enemy."

Dober soon saw that he must make his decision. Going to the governor he announced that he intended to quit his position. "I do not understand you," said the governor. "Do you prefer starving?" But Dober was not to be dissuaded; he rented a tiny house and went back to his scanty diet. Now and then he earned a few pence by acting as a night watchman.

On one such evening as he sat beside a watchman's fire, he unexpectedly heard footsteps. He jumped to his feet and peered into the darkness. Suddenly the approaching stranger called him by name. His heart leaped up within him as he recognized the voice of his old friend Tobias Leopold.

During the long hours of the night the two friends talked. "You are to go back home," Leopold told Dober. "You have been chosen chief elder of Herrnhut." The next thing Leopold said surprised Dober even more. "Eighteen of us have come from Herrnhut; we are to settle on the neighboring island of St. Croix and begin work there. Chamberlain Van Pless of Denmark has promised Zinzendorf that we shall have work there to support ourselves and complete freedom to preach to the slaves."

The Great Dying

Dober said a reluctant farewell to his friends and started back to Herrnhut. For several months the new missionaries remained in St. Thomas. During their stay two of the men and one of the women fell sick and died. On September 1, 1734, the group took a small boat for nearby St. Croix. One of the children died on the short journey and so their first service in their new home was a funeral service. Drinking water was scarce. What water the missionaries could find was often polluted, and men and women did not know in those days how dangerous polluted water can be. One after another became sick, and one after another died; in three months only nine of the original eighteen were left. In January 1735 Tobias Leopold died. On February 20 eleven more men and women left Herrnhut for St. Croix (no news of the first group had yet reached Herrnhut). When the second group arrived in May they found all the remaining members of the first group sick in bed. Within six weeks four of the newcomers had died also. About this time news of what had taken place reached Herrnhut, and orders were sent by the first boat for everyone to return home. Of the twenty-nine who had left Herrnhut with such complete devotion, only eight lived to return home. Down through the years this tragic story in Moravian history has been called by the name the little town of Herrnhut first gave it, "Das Grosse Sterben," or, as we would say in English, "The Great Dying."

My Hens for the Gospel

Was the work begun with such high and holy courage to end in such bitter tragedy?

No! On March 23, 1736, Frederick Martin arrived in St. Thomas. Yes, he had been told all about "Das Grosse Sterben," but back in old Moravia he had been imprisoned for his faith. One foggy night he had managed to outwit his guards; ten days later he had arrived in Herrnhut. The faith for which he had suffered was dear to him, and the call to spread it could not be denied, death or no death.

On his first Sunday in Tappus he took a walk. Seeing a Negro lad he asked: "Would you like to hear about the Savior who loves us?"

The Negro's eyes lit up. "Yes," he said. "If you will tell me about him, I will give you my two hens."

Knowing well that the poor slave probably owned nothing more than the hens, Martin said, "I will not take your hens. Come to my house tonight."

The young slave came and the missionary talked to him of Jesus and his love. When at last the slave had to return home, Frederick Martin had won his first convert. As he thought about the events of the evening he said to himself, "The best thing for me to do is to go around from one plantation to another and speak to the slaves one by one and make sure that every one understands what I say."

The result of this decision was that within six months 200 slaves had become Christians. The missionary's little house was crowded every night in the week. On September 30, 1736 the first three converts were baptized by a Moravian minister (Augustus Spangenberg, later a bishop), who had come from Herrnhut on an official visit. The converts were named Peter, Andrew, and Nathaniel. The seed sown at such great cost had begun to bear fruit.

"Gens Aeterna"

The public baptism of three slaves, on the plantation of a friendly planter named Carstens, attracted a great deal of attention. Although a few planters and officials had supported the mission from the beginning, the vast majority were now very angry. An attempt was made to burn down Martin's house. Drunken men were sent to break up his meetings. When such threats failed the planters concocted another scheme. Frederick Martin, they said, was not a genuine minister; he had been ordained by mail. This last part was true; for after he had made a number of converts, Bishop Nitschmann had sent him a letter from Herrnhut "ordaining" him. The planters, however, ignored the fact that proper notice of this ordination had been sent to both the governor of St. Thomas and the king of Denmark. This make-believe minister, said the planters, was actually baptizing people and conducting communion services. With a great show of piety the planters protested to the governor that they could not endure such sacrilege. "Wishing to content the people," the governor put Martin, his fellow worker Freundlich, and Freundlich's wife in prison.

For several months the missionaries sweltered in the stuffy little jail. They would probably have died if the friendly planter Carstens had not sent them food. Negro converts surrounded the prison every evening and Martin preached through the bars of his little window. "I intend to hold out to the end," he wrote home to Herrnhut, "and trust God to turn everything to his praise."

Then one day startling news began going the rounds on the island: "Count Zinzendorf is coming!" When the planters heard this they quickly lost some of their blustery courage. They remembered having heard that Zinzendorf was on good terms with the king of Denmark and they began wondering how the king would feel about what they had done.

As the vessel bearing the count neared the island, he stood upon the deck looking at the white sand and the yellow rocks as Dober and Nitschmann had done a few years before. Standing with him were the Webers and Mr. and Mrs. Lohans. Turning to them Zinzendorf asked, "What if we find no one? Suppose our missionaries are dead?"

"Then we are here," said Missionary Weber. "Gens Aeterna (a people that will not die), these Moravians!" cried the count.

"I Have Come to See You"

Within a few hours Zinzendorf had landed. Seeing a Negro near the fort he asked, "Where are the missionaries?"

"They are in jail."

"For how long?"

"More than three months."

"What are the Negroes doing now?"

"We go to the prison and the missionaries preach through the window. There are more Christians now than ever."

What happened then can best be told in the count's own words: "I burst into the castle (the governor's residence) like thunder!"

Soon the missionaries were out of jail. The governor apologized, saying that he had been practically forced to do what he had done. From now on, he promised, the missionaries would not be harmed. Martin would be permitted to preach and to teach and to do everything except perform marriages. When Zinzendorf showed the governor a letter from the king of Denmark authorizing the Moravians to do mission work in the West Indies, the governor gave in on this matter also.

For three weeks Zinzendorf held open-air meetings up and down the island. "St. Thomas," he wrote home, "is a greater marvel than Herrnhut." Four centers of work were laid out and the first church officers appointed. When the time for his return arrived the count addressed a great crowd of Christians. "I have come all this way to see you," he said, "and I rejoice to see such a good beginning made. It is what I have longed for these last six years since I first sent my brethren to you. Thank God that he has so richly blessed Martin and his fellow workers. . . .I rejoice to see that the cross of Christ is known on more than fifty plantations. . . .The king of Denmark will be delighted to hear that in his dominions the heathen are learning to know the one true God. Still greater will be the joy of Jesus, who knows the heart of every one of you."

How Frederick Martin Went Home

For fourteen years Frederick Martin toiled faithfully among the slaves. With his own hands he felled trees and erected schools and chapels. Up and down the island and into neighboring islands he carried the gospel. At fifty years of age he was an old man. One day in St. Croix, after being caught in a terrible rainstorm, he came home and went to bed. After a few days of fever he said to his wife, "Dear heart, I am going to the Savior. You must still keep bright and cheerful. I am happier than I can tell you. All I ask is that you request the governor to allow me to be buried on the Princess plantation, near the schoolhouse."

The dying missionary's request was granted; loving hands prepared his grave. Hundreds of Negroes attended the funeral service. So great was the weeping that at last no one could continue the service and the people went home.

Today the place where the schoolhouse stood is dense woodland, but faithful Christians keep a little space cleared around the white stone which marks the hero's grave. When the 200th anniversary of the beginning of Moravian missions was observed in 1932, a special service was held in this clearing in the woods. Wreaths and flowers were laid upon the grave and there was a hymn and a prayer. The Secretary of Missions, who had come from London to participate in the services, wrote: "As we stood there, we were seeing a brave and solitary man, patiently and in the face of illness going about among the people, telling them of Christ in whose service he was working, gathering around him a company of simple, earnest Christian folk and laying the foundation of Christ's Kingdom in the Islands."

The Virgin Islands

From the humble beginnings on St. Thomas and St. Croix the Moravians soon carried the gospel to St. John, the third of the three islands which (with some sixty tiny islands) constitute today's Virgin Islands.

On St. Thomas stands the impressive Memorial church, located on Charlotte Amalie's main street. A modern parsonage has been built in the hills near New Herrnhut, where Frederick Martin purchased the first land as a site for the mission he had come to establish. Here stands the New Herrnhut church, oldest Moravian church in the New World. Several miles from Memorial church, on the other side of the city is the Nisky congregation, where ancient facilities have been replaced with modern buildings. In September 1971 a thousand persons squeezed into Nisky's new air-conditioned church when it was dedicated by Bishop Peter Gubi, veteran Moravian missionary and administrator.

On St. Croix there are three congregations: Frederiksted and Christiansted (names which remind us of the Danish background of these islands) and Midlands, near the center of the island. In recent years these congregations have renovated their buildings, and a youth camp has been established at Christiansted.

The little island of St. John, more than half of which is now a national park, has two churches. The minister lives on a hill at Emmaus overlooking the sea; he travels over the hills to Bethany church, closer to the tourist area. But even though Emmaus is now at the quieter end of the island staunch friends of the mission have provided a new manse and brought electricity to the Moravian buildings.

Crumpled Paper Island

An old story has it that when someone asked Columbus, who is said to have visited Jamaica in May 1494, what the island was like, he took a piece of paper, crumpled it in his hand and laid it down upon the table.

Moravians, the first Christian missionaries to come to this tropical paradise, arrived in 1754, in response to the invitation of two planters who presented them with a plantation to use as a base for mission work. This was a generous gift, but two facts cast dark shadows upon the mission. The first was that slaves on a plantation were considered a part of the property; this made the missionaries slave owners, and slaves had learned to expect nothing good of their masters. In the second place, the plantation was in the swampy lowlands and one missionary after another died in the unhealthy spot.

However, when John Ellis came, in 1824, he moved the mission into the healthy hill country where Fairfield was founded. A friendly planter paid for new buildings. Then, in 1838, Jamaican slaves were freed. Thus the two worst enemies of the mission, disease and slavery, were overcome. When the first centenary of the mission was celebrated in 1854, there were thirteen stations and 4,000 converts.

In 1861, Bethlehem College was opened with three pupils, as a training school for women teachers. Today it is a well developed training college and receives grants from the Jamaican and other governments to further its work. The Moravian Church is also one of the sponsors of the United Theological College of the West Indies, in Kingston, and candidates for the Moravian ministry of several provinces receive their training here.

With fifty-five congregations on the island, the Jamaican province has been able to establish their own church camp, called Camp Hope, and the province is responsible for new work begun on the Grand Cayman Island.

Hangings Every Monday

The first Moravian missionary on Antigua was Samuel Isles, who arrived in 1756. He found conditions among the slaves deplorable. Many of them were endeavoring to drown their troubles in drink. Fighting, stabbing, and poisoning were the order of the day. Since the planters could not be bothered with separating the innocent from the guilty, they simply rounded up the worst offenders every Monday morning and hanged them.

In 1769 Peter Brown came to the island. When he arrived there were but fourteen converts. When "Massa Brown" died in 1791 there were more than 7,000. Such an impact did the early missionaries have upon the island that planters were led to free their slaves in 1834, four years before an Act of Parliament decreed such freedom.

From 1958, extensive rebuilding has been done in all of the congregations on the island, and today all of the churches are of stone or block construction. New congregations are being organized and work begun on a youth camp site at Gracebay, where an historic old school building remains. Strong local leadership provides a good base for church extension and ongoing ministry.

On the Bearded Island

Portuguese explorers gave Barbados its name (meaning "bearded") from a native tree with drooping, mossy branches.

Of the first three missionaries to come to the island, in 1765, two died of fever within a month. The third, completely disheartened, withdrew from mission service. In 1780, a hurricane destroyed the buildings a second group of missionaries had erected. Not until after slavery had been abolished, in 1834, was genuine progress made. Even then there were setbacks such as the cholera epidemic of 1854 in which thousands of persons died, but during these terrible times "the missionaries lived out the love they had proclaimed as they ministered to their people," and that kind of seed always produces a harvest. Today there are a dozen congregations on the island. The newest one is at Bethlehem, established in 1971.

In 1965 the bicentenary of the mission was observed. A thousand persons gathered in Calvary church for a service of thanksgiving and praise.

Going After the Moravians

In 1776 a planter named John Gardiner journeyed to London to invite the Moravians to send missionaries to preach to the slaves on St. Kitts. When two men came, Gardiner gave them a house in Basseterre, the capital town. Here the first church was erected in 1795. By 1800 there were two thousand

Moravians on the island. In spite of earthquakes, floods, riots, an invasion by the French, and times of economic distress when the price of sugar fell, the work has continued to grow. In recent years, the little group of four congregations, constantly handicapped by a shortage of ministers, has nevertheless extended the work at Basseterre, the main station.

Trinidad and Tobago

At the southern end of the chain of West Indian islands are Trinidad and Tobago.

The first Moravian missionary in Tobago was John Montgomery, father of the poet James Montgomery. His efforts were rudely interrupted by the riots which occurred during the French occupation in the 1790s. It was 1827 before a second attempt was made. In that year planter Hamilton, who had been John Montgomery's friend, welcomed Mr. and Mrs. Peter Ricksecker of Bethlehem, Pennsylvania, to the island. Soon a station named Montgomery grew up. Moriah was established in 1842, Spring Gardens in 1853; Bon Accord, Black Rock, and Bethesda followed before the end of the century.

In 1963 Hurricane Flora leveled 75 percent of the island's buildings, and four of the congregations replaced their buildings in the following five years. Black Rock completed a new building in 1976 and a new work was started at Mount Thomas in the 1972.

In 1890 a Swiss Moravian, Marc Richard, went to Trinidad to minister to West Indies who had gone there in search of work on sugar, cocoa and coconut plantations. Within fifteen years half a dozen congregations had been established, but the distance between the congregations on this large island and a constant shortage of ministers have hindered normal growth in membership and self-support.

In 1907 a native minister was asked to go to the Dominican Republic to care for Moravians there. In 1960 the little Moravian congregation in this area joined the Dominican Evangelical Church.

Guyana

Several attempts, going back as far as 1738, to establish Christian work in Guyana had failed, because of opposition from planters, insurrections, and the unhealthy climate of the areas selected. The present work in Guyana may be said to have begun in 1878 when a friendly planter offered to pay the salaries of a Moravian minister and a teacher.

During the first half of its history, Moravian work in what was then British Guiana reached its height under the leadership of the Rev. John Dingwall, whose forty-seven years of service saw the firm establishment of the Georgetown congregation, and the Comenius Day School with as many as a thousand pupils. Continuing his work until he was past eighty-five years of age and completely blind, he died having laid firm foundations for the future. "All British Guiana revered John Dingwall" said the Georgetown *Daily Chronicle.*

For some years following Dingwall's death, the lack of funds and personnel hindered further growth. Then, in 1958, American Moravians began giving assistance. Church buildings were rebuilt or renovated; programs of leadership training and stewardship were launched. The coming of independence to Guyana at midnight on May 25, 1966, produced problems, but was also a challenge to the church. In spite of staffing problems, political constraints, and theological divisions, the province reported eight congregations and many areas for growth at the Unity Synod of 1988.

Chapter 7

The First Century of Missions

Now that we have seen how our church became a missionary church and surveyed the work in the area in which Moravian missions began, we shall turn to the other lands into which Moravians carried the gospel during the hundred years which followed the days of Dober and Nitschmann.

"Greenland's Icy Mountains"

This great missionary hymn has a special meaning for Moravians, for it was to faraway Greenland that three missionaries sailed early in 1733, less than half a year after Dober and Nitschmann had started for the West Indies. The three were Christian David and two cousins, Matthew and Christian Stach. Upon their arrival the newcomers were warmly welcomed by Hans Egede, a Norwegian missionary who had been in Greenland about ten years. The Danish government had sent him, hoping that mission work might civilize the Eskimos and lead to the opening up of trade. He had learned the language, painted gospel pictures, and preached faithfully year after year, but without winning more than a few converts. Whenever they could, the natives stole the missionary's fish hooks and equipment. When he talked to them of God, they laughed and jeered, "Show him to us!" The Danish government was just about to recall the discouraged missionary. Although Matthew Stach wrote home bravely enough, "The darkness in Greenland must give way to light," five long years were to pass before the first rays of the dawn were seen.

"Kanok Ipa?"

It was on the evening of June 2, 1738, that the great joy came. Missionary John Beck was patiently translating the gospels into Eskimo while a group of curious natives sat around watching.

"What is the book about?" asked an Eskimo.

After thinking a moment the missionary asked, "Do you have souls?"

"Yes," said some of the men.

"When you die, where will your souls go?" asked the missionary.

"Up to the sky," said some.

"Down into the ground," said others.

The missionary breathed a prayer. Suddenly a voice said to his heart. "Read to them from the book."

John Beck began at the top of the page he was translating—the twenty-sixth chapter of Matthew—and read the story of Christ praying in Gethsemane. All at once an Eskimo, Kajarnak by name, sprang up. "Kanok Ipa?" he cried. "How is that? Read me that again!"

Thus it came about that what theological arguments had been unable to do, "the old, old story of Jesus and his love" accomplished. In a Moravian museum in England there is preserved today the very Bible from which John Beck was translating when the first Eskimo looked in faith to Jesus and believed.

Soon Kajarnak (who was given the name Samuel) was baptized. He lived for only two years after his conversion, but he filled those years with work for the Lord he had come to love. Up and down the coast he went with the missionaries, adding his witness to their words. As he lay dying he said to his family and friends, "I am the first of you that turned to the Savior, and now it is his will that I should be the first to go to him. If you are faithful to him, we shall see one another again and rejoice forever."

In 1747 the first permanent building was erected, containing a chapel and six rooms for the missionaries. It was prefabricated in Holland and shipped to Greenland in sections. When it was erected it was the largest building the Eskimos had ever seen and for years it was a thing of wonder to the natives.

Within a few years a little chain of mission stations was established along the Greenland coast. When Matthew Stach went home to Herrnhut in 1771, a thousand Eskimos had become Christians.

For 170 years Moravians preached the gospel in Greenland. By that time almost all the Eskimos living along the bleak coast had been Christianized. The Moravians, therefore, in 1899 turned their stations over to the Lutheran Church which had congregations throughout the settled portions of the great island.

To the American Indians

Early in April 1735 a little vessel, *The Two Brothers*, entered the Savannah River below the little Georgia town of the same name. On board were ten Moravians who had come, under the leadership of Spangenberg, to preach the gospel to the American Indians and establish a settlement in the New World to which Moravians might flee if they were ordered out of Saxony.

The trustees of the Georgia colony had given the Moravians a number of lots in and around the town of Savannah. The settlers planted gardens, worked as carpenters and builders, and endeavored to contact Indian tribes in the area. In February 1736 a second group of twenty-five men and women arrived. It was on this voyage that John and Charles Wesley first met the Moravians and became impressed by their calmness during a great storm. John Wesley never tired of telling the story: When a mighty wave split the mainsail and threatened to swallow the little ship, "a terrible screaming began among the English. The Germans (he meant the Moravians) sang calmly on.

"I asked one of them afterward, `Were you not afraid?'

"He answered, `I thank God, no!'

"I asked,`But were not your women and children afraid?'

"He replied, `Our women and children are not afraid to die.'"

When Wesley arrived in Savannah, Governor Oglethorpe introduced him to Spangenberg. Spangenberg had been a university professor, and he and Wesley soon became firm friends. Thus began a contact which was to lead to great results. Three years later, back in London, Wesley went to a little Moravian prayer meeting in Aldersgate Street and "felt his heart strangely warmed." Wesley always referred to this experience as his conversion. For the first time in his life the faith of his mind became the faith of his heart also.

For a while the Moravian colony prospered. In 1737 a school was established for Indians of the Lower Creek tribe. The settlers were organized into a congregation, and one of them, Anton Seiffert, was ordained to become minister of the flock.

A few years later, however, the whole brave experiment came to an end. Savannah was on the frontier between the English colonies and Spanish Florida, and wars between these two great powers had repercussions even in faraway America. The Spaniards dreamed of pushing northward; the English in Georgia were determined to prevent this. Little Savannah was like a fortress and all its citizens were soldiers—all that is, except the Moravians, who calmly announced that they did not believe in fighting. Such "lack of patriotism" soon caused them to be suspected and even hated by their neighbors. What was even worse, sickness began taking its toll. During 1737, for instance, eight members of the little colony died. In 1740 evangelist George Whitefield visited Savannah, and when he offered to take the Moravians to Pennsylvania with him, they were happy to accept his offer.

In later years the trustees of the Georgia colony expressed regret that they had permitted the Moravians to leave. Today a monument in the city of Savannah marks the fact of their settlement.

South America (1735)

In 1735, when the first Moravians arrived in Paramaribo, capital of the Dutch colony of Surinam, they found the country inhabited by Dutch planters, their Negro slaves, and Arawack Indians, who lived in the jungles. When the missionaries attempted to preach to the slaves, as they had done in the West Indies, they found the opposition of both planters and government officials so bitter that they pushed a hundred miles into the jungle and settled in the heart of the Indian country. In the swampy, fever-infested jungle their work was most difficult. One missionary after another died. The Arawack language was so difficult that some of them gave up hope of ever learning it, and in spite of all that was being sacrificed for them, many of the Indians simply trusted no one whose face was white. Yet missionary Schumann, one of the pioneers, baptized 400 Arawacks before he fell, a victim of fever, at the age of forty.

The Negroes in the Bush (1765)

During the years in which the missionaries were working against such difficulties in the Arawack country, a strange thing was happening along the coast. Negro slaves were escaping in increasing numbers from the bitter life of plantations and making their way into the swamps and jungles of the interior. Several times the planters sent bands of soldiers to round up the escaped slaves, but poisoned arrows and jungle snakes soon put an end to such expeditions. At last, in 1765, the government decided to make peace with the Negroes in the bush and signed a treaty with them. Up to this time both planters and government officials had treated the Moravians with contempt. Now, however, they were properly frightened by the obvious power of the Negroes, and in their fear they appealed to the Moravians to civilize the bush Negroes.

Soon a mission station was opened on the Surinam River, another on the Senthea Creek. One day Arabi, king of the Negroes in that area, came to visit the missionary. Missionary Stoll told him of the Son of God who had died for the sins of all people.

"I have never done anything wrong," said Arabi.

The missionary made no comment on that. "What is that in your hand?" he asked.

"My god," said Arabi, holding up a stick adorned with parrot feathers.

"A stick cannot do anything for you," said the missionary.

Arabi went home, thinking about what the missionary had said. All at once he said to his god-stick, "I am going to throw you into the fire. If you are a god, the fire will not hurt you; if you burn up, the white man is right." The result of this courageous experiment was that King Arabi became a Christian. For fifty years (1771-1821) he assisted the missionaries in every way, and at times he even preached the gospel himself.

As the years passed, the old enemy, disease, continued to take its toll and many more missionaries died. Soon the bush country came to be known as "Dedde Kondre" (country of death). There came a period of twenty-five years in which not one missionary's voice was heard in the jungle.

A Messenger Named John

In 1857 there came to the missionary in Paramaribo a bush Negro who said that his name was John King. He had come from a completely heathen village. No one knew of any missionaries who had ever visited his area. Yet he announced that an "angel" had spoken to him and told him to go to the Moravian missionary in Paramaribo. Missionary Van Calker questioned John at some length and at last said, "It was the Lord Jesus who spoke to you. Stay with me for a time and I will teach you about him."

When John King went home he took with him a New Testament, a hymnal, and a catechism. Three years passed before he returned to say that he had built a church in his village and that he had come to receive further instruction and be baptized. When the missionaries accompanied him to his village, they found the church, and soon a congregation of Christians had been organized. For thirty years John King continued to guide his people into the truth. Shortly before he died a missionary wrote: "It is impossible to look at his face without a feeling of affection and emotion."

At midnight on June 23, 1863, emancipation came to the 50,000 slaves in Surinam, about half of them Moravians. Missionary Van Calker wrote later that when the clock struck midnight "the moment overwhelmed me; it threw me to my knees to thank the Lord."

As the years passed the church spread from Paramaribo into the interior. Today there are 35,000 Moravians in the city, gathered into a dozen congregations, and as many more in about forty congregations outside of the capital city. The church worked not only among Negroes, but among Indonesians, Javanese, and Chinese. It maintains schools and orphanages. The Bethesda Leper Colony goes back to 1897; the Princess Juliana hospital was opened in Kabel in 1948; in 1965 a second hospital was begun in the interior.

In 1963, Surinam became a province of the Unity and 2,500 people attended the lovefeast commemorating the event. The chairman of the country's legislature, himself a Moravian, began his address with the words, "Brethren and sisters in Christ."

From Surinam the work of the church has spread into the islands of Curacao and Aruba.

Into the Dark Continent (1737)

When the Moravians were asked to send missionaries to the unhappy slaves of South Africa, George Schmidt volunteered to go. Like many another Herrnhuter, he had escaped from prison back in old Moravia and made his way to the new town. To the end of his life his ankles were marked by the scars the cruel prison chains had made. In February 1736 he set out for Amsterdam, en route to South Africa.

In Amsterdam it was the old story of discouragement and ridicule. Try as he could, a whole year passed before he could get passage to Africa. He found when he reached Cape Town that no one in the city had any kind words for missionaries, so he went fifty miles into the interior and settled among the despised Hottentots. The Hottentots had once been an independent people, but Dutch traders had invaded their villages, seized all they desired as slaves, and driven the children and the aged into the woods.

Finding their language difficult, the missionary did an interesting thing: he decided to teach the natives to speak Dutch! He opened a school and soon had fifty pupils. The kindness of the missionary conquered the fear of the people. On March 31, 1742, Willem, the first convert, was baptized. "I know I am not yet what I ought to be," he told the missionary, "but I will abide with Jesus."

When planters and officials in Cape Town heard what missionary Schmidt was doing, they were almost insane with anger. It took them almost a year to accomplish it, but the order came from the government: the missionary must leave Africa at once.

Back home George Schmidt worked as an evangelist, waiting in vain for the door to Africa to open again. As the years passed he prayed on. On August 1, 1785, he was found dead upon his knees at his bed, praying for his beloved Africa.

"The Savior Has Not Forgotten"

"Africa once shielded the infant Jesus," wrote Dr. Thompson in his book *Moravian Missions*, "and our ascended Savior has not forgotten that continent."

In 1792 the directors of the Dutch East India Company elected a new president, who permitted the Moravians to send missionaries again to South Africa. Soon three Moravians landed at Cape Town, and after inquiring around they found persons who knew where Schmidt's mission had been. When they arrived at the spot, now called Bavianskloof (Monkey Valley) they found a part of the wall of Schmidt's house and a great pear tree the missionary had planted. Best of all, they found an old woman named Magdalene, who remembered the brave pioneer.

"Did George Schmidt baptize you?" the new missionaries asked.

"Yes, masters."

"Did he tell you about Jesus?"

"Yes," said the aged woman. "I remember that. He told me about Jesus and gave me a book."

"May we see the book?"

Magdalene brought them the little Dutch New Testament George Schmidt had given her fifty years before. Today that little book is preserved in the mission at Gnadendal (Valley of Grace), the new name the missionaries gave the place. It is kept in a little box made from the wood of George Schmidt's pear tree.

For five years the missionaries preached beneath the pear tree before the first church was erected. In 1800 this building was replaced by another which seated 1,500 people.

Bullets or the Gospel

In 1828 a Kaffir chief in the eastern part of South Africa made a strange request of Lord Somerset, then British governor of the province: "I fear for my life. Please send soldiers to protect me."

The governor replied, "Missionaries are better than soldiers. I will ask the Moravians to come to your country." When he approached the Moravians the governor promised that if they would go into Kaffraria he would help to pay the cost of establishing a mission station.

The early days of the mission were difficult ones. In the fierce wars between various tribes, mission buildings were often burned. One time a savage chief and his men met their match, for when they arrived at a mission station and prepared to burn it to the ground, a native Christian woman, Wilhelmina Stompjes, calmly ordered them to leave. The chief was stunned; he was angry to think that a woman would dare to give him orders. But when Wilhelmina blocked his path, he turned around and led his men away. When Governor Sir Harry Smith visited the mission a few years later, he said, "I have been in many fine churches, but my heart has never been so touched as it was in this humble temple of God in the wilderness in which black people and white people sit side by side as brethren in Christ."

East Africa

In 1889 Moravians in Germany learned with joy that a man named Daniel Krakau had left the Moravian Church $200,000 for missionary work. General Synod decided that half of this amount should be used to begin a new mission in German East Africa. Early in 1891, Theodore Meyer and three companions established the first station in the new field. Almost six years passed without a convert. Then a heathen woman confessed her faith and was baptized and given the name Numwagile (I have found him). Soon her son was baptized also, and from this beginning the mission spread in every direction.

From the early days of the mission, native workers have been prominent. One day missionary Meyer saw a fine-looking young man leading a native dance.

"Wouldn't you like to be a teacher?" asked the missionary.

"Yes," replied the native. The missionary began teaching him and soon had him conducting a school. Several years passed before he asked the missionary to tell him more about Jesus, but in 1912 he was baptized, receiving the name of Sakaria. In 1935 he was ordained a minister.

During World War I this promising mission received a serious blow. Most of the missionaries had come from Germany; therefore, they were ordered home and mission property was taken over by British officials. But in 1920, when it seemed as if all had been lost, the Free Church of Scotland sent missionaries into the territory. These faithful men and women repaired the damaged properties of the Moravian mission (there had been an earthquake in 1919), gathered the scattered Christians together, and renewed the work.

When German Moravians were permitted to return to Africa in 1926, the Free Church turned the whole field back to them, refusing payment of any kind for salaries or repairs they had made. For this gracious gift of love the Moravian Church owes the Free Church of Scotland a great debt of gratitude. When the Moravians returned, they found that the little flock they had left had increased to 5,000 in the intervening years.

"Welcome to the Moravians!"

A thousand Africans marched out of the village of Urambo in East Central Africa one day in January in 1898 to welcome two Moravian missionaries and their wives. The London Missionary Society had asked the Moravians to take over their station in this area. Two hundred volunteers had come with them to help them get established, for this new field was so far from other Moravian centers in Africa that it was going to have to stand on its own feet from the beginning.

The courage and faith of the pioneers was justified. Three years later a second station was opened and five more stations were begun within the next ten years. The work has continued to grow steadily in spite of disastrous fires at several stations, the internment of missionaries during World War I, and other troubles.

In 1923, Dr. and Mrs. A. J. Keevil began work among lepers. The little house in which they started has grown into the Kidugalo Leper Settlement, which is affiliated with the Moravian Hospital in Sikonge. When Christians in the leper colony celebrated their first communion in 1936, the doctor felt that individual cups should be used for the service. Since none were available the missionary's wife supplied egg cups for the service. Later hearing of this, a member of the London Association sent a communion set to the settlement.

One of the lepers wrote a letter of thanks: "Very much thanks, our fathers, for the cups of fellowship we have now received. When we saw them we were all delighted. . . .We are grateful in the name of our Savior Jesus Christ; may he exalt his name among his people!"

Phenomenal Growth and Progress

The former two provinces in Tanzania have now become four with an influx of people from neighboring countries. The church has faced challenges which have demanded new structures, more leadership, and greater resources. Other provinces of the Moravian Church have assisted by sending medical personnel, teachers for the theological schools, and financial support to assist with new buildings and programs. The Tanzania provinces work together in supporting the Theological School at Mbeya and attempt to assist one another in other ministries.

The four Tanzania provinces reported phenomenal church growth at the 1988 Unity Synod and also shared plans for further expansion in Tanzania, Zaire, Malawi, and Zambia. The four provinces currently embrace nearly half the membership of the worldwide Moravian Church.

Along the Labrador Coast

Encouraged by the success of the Greenland mission, the Moravians sent John Ehrhardt and three companions, in 1752, to Labrador. English merchants who were anxious to establish trade contacts offered to take the missionaries and a prefabricated house to the distant land.

In July the missionaries landed and erected their house. Then everyone sailed up the coast looking for Eskimo villages; when one was sighted the captain, Ehrhardt, and four sailors got into a little boat and went ashore. They were never seen again. Many historians say flatly that they were murdered; others insist they must have drowned in the icy waters. After waiting for a week the frightened sailors got their boat back to the spot at which they had erected the house. When the mate pleaded with the missionaries to help him get his ship back to England, they felt obliged to do this.

"Our Friend Has Come!"

A dozen years passed before a second attempt was made. Then in 1764 Jens Haven, who had served in Greenland for six years, volunteered to go to Labrador. In Newfoundland he persuaded a French captain to take him to Labrador. When the first village was sighted, the captain cast anchor and waited. Eskimos in their kayaks soon swarmed around. Jens Haven leaned over the side of the ship and called to the Eskimos in the language he had learned in Greenland, "Come up to the boat. I have something to tell you. I am your friend."

"Our friend has come!" the Eskimos shouted to one another. Forthwith they invited Haven to come to the land with them. The captain protested loudly; the little missionary hesitated. Years later he wrote, "I confidently turned to the Lord in prayer and thought, `I will go with them in thy name. If they kill me, my work on earth will be done and I shall be with thee; if they spare my life, I shall firmly believe it to be thy will that they should hear and receive the gospel.' I accordingly went, and as soon as we arrived on shore, all of them sent up a shout, `Our friend has come!'"

Jens Haven returned to London with a happy heart. The Society for the Furtherance of the Gospel, which had been established a few years before, agreed to support a mission in Labrador and the next summer the first group of missionaries was on its way. A few years later, in order to guarantee food and supplies for the mission, the society (which soon became the official mission agency of English Moravians) bought the *Jersey Packet*. This little boat was the first in a long line of Moravian mission ships, twelve in all, which for 150 years made the dangerous voyage from London to Labrador at least once a year. The last five ships were all called the *Harmony* and this name became well known throughout the shipping world. Whenever the ship sailed there was a farewell service on board; when she returned (in early years a round trip took six months) there was a service of thanksgiving. Even during the blockade of Britain in World War I, the German navy was instructed, "Let the Moravian mission ship *Harmony* go through!"

In 1926 the Moravian Church sold her trading rights to the Hudson's Bay Company, which, with its fleet of ships and worldwide contacts, was glad to guarantee delivery of supplies to our Labrador mission and even free passage for missionaries.

At one time the Moravians had as many as ten centers of work in Labrador, but in recent years Eskimos have been gradually abandoning northern settlements and moving to the more southerly areas of the country. At present, Moravian work is concentrated in five areas. One of the newer stations is at Happy Valley, where a large town has grown up around the Canadian-American air base at Goose Bay. There are Grenfell hospitals at Northeast River and Makkovik stations. Hopedale has a U.S. radar base. The fifth station is Nain, oldest of all, established in 1771.

Outward conditions have changed greatly during the last decade or two. Today a visitor finds government plants for freezing fish, modern schools, even high schools under government supervision, telephone service in many small villages, and cars lining up in front of the Happy Valley church on a Sunday morning. In this town our church cooperated with the Episcopalians a few years ago in the erection of a school.

In August 1971 the Labrador mission celebrated its 200th anniversary. The

Memorial University of Newfoundland took this opportunity to honor the Rev. F. W. Peacock, veteran Moravian missionary and superintendent, by conferring upon him the degree of Doctor of Literature.

Grand Failures

During the first century of their missions the Moravians went not only to the West Indies, Greenland, and the other lands of which we have written. They also went to many places in which they found it impossible to establish permanent work. In 1734 they were in Lapland; two years later they were roughly expelled from St. Petersburg, Russia. In 1736 they went to the Gold Coast of Africa. When this undertaking failed they tried again in 1768. Within a few months every one of the nine missionaries died, another "Grosse Sterben," bringing this venture to a tragic end.

In 1739 Abraham Richter died in faraway Algiers while attempting to found a mission. A year later Arved Gradin was thrown out of Constantinople. In Persia Moravian missionaries were robbed and beaten; in Egypt John Antes was bastinadoed (beaten upon the soles of the feet, a torture which frequently caused death by bleeding from the ears). Missionary Antes survived, but for years could not walk without pain.

They tried in vain, these men and their friends. There is nothing to show for their sacrifice and devotion. And yet—is there not something grand even about their "failures"?

The Advance Guard

One great result of the missionary fervor of the early Moravians must never be forgotten. Their work served to awaken other Protestants to their missionary responsibilities. When the Moravians began their work, not a single Protestant church in all the world was doing mission work, but they were supported either by local societies or wealthy patrons (and in a few cases, as we have seen from the story of Hans Egede, by governments). But as the story of what the Moravians were doing became more and more widely known, other churches began to ask whether "Go into all the world" might not apply to them also.

One example can be given. In 1790 Moravians in England began the publication of a little missionary journal *Periodical Accounts* containing reports from their mission fields. William Carey, a Baptist leader, read the early issues of this paper and his heart was stirred. Coming to a meeting of Baptist ministers, he threw down upon the table half a dozen copies of the journal. "See," he cried, "what these Moravians have done! Should we not follow their example?" The result of Carey's appeal was the establishment of the Baptist Missionary Society.

One more great result of Moravian missions deserves mention. The results of Moravian mission work in the West Indies gave Wilberforce his most powerful argument in favor of the abolition of slavery. When many Englishmen argued that freeing the slaves would only result in having them turn upon white people and "abolish" them, Wilberforce replied, "The Moravians have taught the slaves to respect law and order; they have prepared the slaves to receive the great gift of liberty." History has shown that he was right.

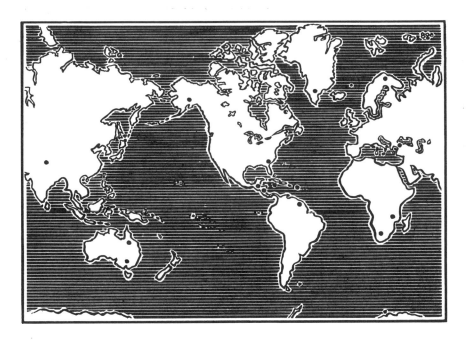

Chapter 8

The Second Hundred Years, and More

When the Moravians celebrated the first centenary of their mission work in 1832, they had forty-one main stations, more than 200 missionaries at work, and more than 45,000 persons belonged to their missions.

The first new field to be entered after the centenary was Nicaragua.

Land for Sale

In 1841 King Robert Charles Frederick of the Miskito coast of Nicaragua gave two British sea captains a large tract of land. When the captains got home, they attempted to dispose of their new property, but no one was interested in it. Not easily discouraged, one of the captains went to Germany, where he interested Prince Karl of Prussia enough to send three men to Nicaragua to see what kind of place it was. When the three returned, they wrote a long book about the land and its people. Another German prince read the book and decided that Nicaragua needed missionaries more than it needed German settlers, so he appealed to the Moravians. The Moravians wrote to two of their missionaries in Jamaica and said "Go to Nicaragua and look over the field and tell us what you think we should do."

Come and Preach to Us

When the Moravian missionaries arrived in Bluefields, they were warmly welcomed by the British consul (this part of Nicaragua was at that time an independent kingdom under British protection). The consul introduced them to the king, who presented them to the members of the Miskito council, which happened to be in session. The missionaries were invited to speak and when they finished, the council members passed a resolution requesting the Moravian Church to begin mission work in their kingdom. On January 4, 1849, a sailing vessel left London for Bluefields, Nicaragua. On board were one hundred convicts, guarded by fifty soldiers, and three Moravian missionaries. After a stormy trip the vessel reached Bluefields on March 14.

The missionaries began their work by organizing a school. They preached to the Creoles, who understood English; then to the Indians on Rama Cay. Three years after they landed, the first church was dedicated in Bluefields. No other organized religious work of any kind was being done along the coast. "The Moravians," says an old record, "were the first to claim this land for the Cross."

The work thus begun by three missionaries has spread all the way up the coast (and into Honduras, as we shall see), and it has crossed the country into the capital city of Managua. The Area Handbook, published in 1970, by the American University in Washington, D.C., reports: "Roughly half of Nicaragua's 65,000 Protestants are Moravians."

Although the first missionaries enjoyed the favor of the Miskito king, they had little influence upon the people until they began pushing up the coast. On June 12, 1855, Jean Paul Jurgensen arrived at Pearl Lagoon. Three days after his arrival an epidemic of cholera broke out. The new missionary boldly visited the sick and administered all the medicine he had. Soon he was a beloved hero, and every ear was open to the gospel he proclaimed. When a hurricane destroyed his church in 1875, loyal Christians promptly rebuilt it.

In 1881 the entire area was swept by a revival. Indians came from villages up and down the coast pleading for missionaries to come into their areas. Again and again the few missionaries told them: "Go home and build a chapel; if you do that we shall come and preach in your village." Within fifteen years seven new main stations had been established. In 1896 the first native of Nicaragua was ordained a Moravian minister.

A Cross and an Open Book

In 1894 the independent Miskito kingdom was annexed by Nicaragua. For a number of years the new government imposed heavy taxes and import duties on all goods sent to the missionaries, insisted that only Spanish be used in the mission schools, and in other ways made church work difficult. The Moravians made the difficult change to Spanish in all their schools, but in spite of this the government closed their schools. When they were permitted to reopen them years later, they strengthened their educational work by establishing a high school in Bluefields. In 1950 a modern concrete building was erected for this school. In 1970 the Bluefields congregation erected another building with twelve classrooms to house the primary (grade) school which is now maintained by the congregation. When this building was dedicated, the governor paid tribute to the Moravians who had come to his country "with the Cross in one hand and an open book in the other." One area of the new building was dedicated to Elizabeth Marx, another area to Thelma Good, two long-term missionary teachers.

In 1933 Dr. A. D. Thaeler Jr. arrived in Nicaragua "with high hopes," as he put it, "and very little cash" to begin medical work. In 1936, the first small clinic gave way to a permanent Thaeler Memorial Hospital, and as the years passed electricity, an X-ray machine, radio-telephone equipment, etc., were added. During 1969 volunteers from the United States, with many Nicaraguan volunteers, erected completely new and modern buildings for the hospital. When the new buildings were opened, the president of Nicaragua and his wife came to visit and everyone cheered as the president escorted the first patient to be admitted into the new hospital.

The revolution which began in 1979 caused tremendous changes for the Moravian Church. Twenty-five thousand members of the Moravian Church were displaced and sent to resettlement areas. Ministers were placed in prison, and half of the congregations experienced disruption of their life. While many of the members have begun moving back to their homes, uncertainty still faces the church, and much rebuilding needs to be done. A hurricane which struck the east coast in late 1988 caused some loss of life and great property loss and the destruction of many of the churches.

Yet in the midst of this turmoil the Nicaraguan Moravian Church began new work in neighboring Costa Rica to the south. Six congregations were organized in five years' time.

Honduras

For a number of years before 1930, when Moravian work in Honduras was formerly begun, Nicaraguan missionaries had occasionally visited areas of the country, and Honduran Indians had at times visited Moravian centers in Nicaragua. When Dr. and Mrs. George Heath, who had once served in Nicaragua, volunteered to begin a mission in Honduras, their offer was joyfully accepted. On November 21, 1930, the corner post of the first building was planted. The building, twenty by thirty feet in size, with a roof of palmetto leaves, was intended to serve as a church and the missionary's home. About eighty Indians attended the first service. A lame woman, Hannah Brodick, was the first convert.

From these humble beginnings the work spread into towns and villages all around. Today the Honduras church has more than twenty-five congregations, and every one of them is served by a national Honduran. What is more, year by year Honduras Moravians ask to be trained as Christian pastors.

In course of time, a boarding school for children could be established at Brus. The church also maintains an extensive clinic at Ahuas (referred to by a visitor as "a mini-hospital"). To this medical center as many as a thousand patients have come in a single month.

One of the most significant aspects of the work in Honduras is the cooperative effort of Mennonites, the United Church of Christ, and the Moravians in agricultural missions. Trained agriculturalists, sent throughout the area, discovered buy experiments that soybeans, black-eyed peas and other vegetables could be grown in Honduras. They introduced disease-resistant rice, hardy varieties of corn and banana plants. They taught local inhabitants how to graft fruit trees. They imported Indian Runner ducklings and Rhode Island Red chickens because they could survive in the country. They imported Brahma bulls, and within a few years the beef stock of the country was greatly improved. They emphasized the importance of pure water, and taught people how to dig good wells. They encouraged the planting of gardens, and rewarded the owner of the best garden in a village by presenting that person a shovel and a hoe.

The revolution in neighboring Nicaragua in the 1970s caused many of the Miskito Indians to escape to find refuge. The influx of Moravians brought new challenges to the Honduras church and new work was established among the refugees with staffing from both Nicaraguan and Honduran ministers. Five new churches were begun in the years between the Unity Synods of 1981 and 1988, representing a six percent growth in the membership of the church. The province assumed full responsibility for its work in the same period.

Australia—Where We Laid Foundations

Moravian mission work was established in Victoria province just before the great gold rush of 1852 broke out. The route to the gold fields passed through mission property. The hundred thousand gold-hungry adventurers who streamed into the area so disrupted the work that was just beginning that the project had to be abandoned.

In 1890 another attempt was made to establish a mission in Australia, this time in North Queensland. The Moravian Church supplied the men and the Presbyterian Church of Australia supplied the finances. Even though the work was begun among some of the most backward and savage people of that land (they preached cannibalism) the gospel bore fruit. In 1918 the Presbyterians took full responsibility for the work which they continue to carry on. Thus in Australia, as in Greenland, our Moravian Church was able to lay the foundation for a work that is now being continued by Christians who are closer to the field of operations.

Roof of the World

For more than a hundred years brave and faithful missionaries of our church have preached the gospel among the Tibetans. Refused permission to enter the closed land of Tibet proper, the early missionaries began work among the Tibetans living high in the mountains of northwest India. At the end of a hundred years of the most difficult kind of labor, the Moravian mission had scarcely 150 members.

Had this been a century of no progress? Judge for yourself: The entire Bible has been translated into Tibetan, thanks to the devoted labor of missionaries Jaeschke, Francke, Marx, and Gergan. For years almost the only journal of any kind to circulate in the land was the little paper the Moravian missionaries printed on their mimeograph. Almost the only clean and decent place in which a traveler could spend the night was the Moravian Inn in Leh, where as many as 4,000 persons stopped in a year. For many years the mission maintained a little hospital where many a Buddhist had his first contacts with Christians.

In 1953 Chinese Communists invaded Tibet, plundering and looting as they advanced. Thousands of Tibetans fled across the mountains into India. A small group of Moravians from the Ladakh area finally found a home in the Indian village of Rajpur. Not far away were other Tibetans and before long the Moravian pastor, the Rev. Eliyah T. Phunthsog, opened a school to teach the adults English. Many of the refugees had been weavers, so the missionary got looms and started them weaving rugs and carpets. The British Mission Board sent money for blacksmithing tools, and other refugees began making beds and gates and railings. Now able to support themselves, the people asked one more favor: "Could you start a school for our children?"

Soon a school began with six children meeting under a tree. When the rains came, the missionary begged the use of an empty house. The little school began to grow, and in 1970 a combined school and hostel with a capacity of 170 pupils was erected. When English bishop John Foy visited Rajpur in 1969, he spoke at a morning service in the school, "sitting cross-legged on the floor and with no shoes on, according to Tibetan custom" and the children sang, in their own language, the universal favorite "Jesus loves me, this I know."

During his visit to north India, the bishop was able to make a trip back into the area from which the refugees had come. There he encouraged the few Moravians still clinging to their old homes and ordained two men so that the work of this small mission might be maintained.

In 1965 the worldwide Moravian Church began supporting the work of the

Moravian Institute, which includes a hostel for boarding students, as well as day students. Today the school has between two and three hundred boarding students and includes a woven-rug industry which helps to support the institution while training young people for future employment.

Plowing on Stone

Two things have made the Tibetan mission work like "plowing on stone," as a missionary once put it. The first is the fact that a new Christian is disowned by his or her Buddhist family. In the early days of the mission some means of support had to be found for every convert.

The second thing which makes Christian work difficult is Buddhist hypocrisy. The lama teaches, "Thou shalt not kill any living thing." When a Buddhist wants to kill a goat, therefore, he stuffs rags into the poor beast's nostrils and waits for the animal to die "a natural death." Since reading books brings merit, a rich Buddhist employs a dozen men who go to work in his library like bees, reading out loud and turning the pages as rapidly as possible. In this way their employer can "read" an entire library in a short time. Since the more prayers a person prays the holier he or she becomes, the Buddhist writes a prayer on a slip of paper, puts it into a prayer wheel and spins the wheel, or lets the wind turn it. Every revolution counts as a prayer.

But even in a stony field some good ground is to be found, and the faithfulness of these Christians, who in spite of opposition without and within their country, continue their loyal allegiance to Jesus Christ, must certainly be an encouragement to Christians everywhere.

Alaska—Will the Moravians Go?

In 1794 an Englishman, George Vancouver, sailed into the unknown north Pacific upon a tour of exploration. He landed somewhere near the site of the present city of Sitka, Alaska. When he went ashore he found that a Russian, Alexander Baranov, had been there years before and established a trading post. Alaska had already been discovered. In 1867 Russia, lacking the money to develop trade, gladly sold the territory to the United States for $7,200,000.

Shortly after Alaska came into the possession of the United States the Presbyterians began a mission near Sitka. When Dr. Sheldon Jackson, their mission secretary, visited Alaska, he was impressed by the fact that no church was at work in the vast western area. After appealing in vain to several denominations he contacted the Moravians, who invited him to come to Bethlehem and tell his story in Central Church. There, on February 10, 1884, he asked the question, "Will the Moravians come forward as of old to the help of the Lord in this far-off northern land?"

The next morning five students in the theological seminary volunteered to go to Alaska, and within a few days church authorities voted to begin a mission there.

A few months later the Rev. Adolph Hartman, an experienced missionary among the Indians in Canada, and the Rev. William H. Weinland, one of the five volunteers, were on their way to Alaska with instructions to find a suitable site for a new mission. On May 16 a little vessel landed them at Unalaska. From there they went to Nushagak, where a Greek Catholic priest suggested that they go to the Kuskokwim River district. No one, he told them, was doing any Christian work in that vast area.

Go Up to Bethel

On June 14 Hartman wrote in his diary, "We are now in the mouth of the River Kuskokwim." On June 20 a trading village was sighted. "We were greatly cheered," wrote the missionary, "by the view of this station, situated on a high bank, with a background of pine forest. The text for the day was very encouraging and remarkable: 'God said to Jacob, Arise, go up to Bethel, and dwell there, and make there an altar unto God.' It seemed as if the Lord was speaking to us. . .and pointing out the place for our future operations."

In the summer of 1885 Weinland came back to Bethel with his bride. Accompanying him were a classmate John Kilbuck and his bride, and Hans Torgerson, a Norwegian carpenter who had volunteered to build the first station and help the missionaries get started. A few weeks after they arrived Torgerson slipped on a bundle of wet shingles, fell off their little boat, and was drowned in the cold waters of the Kuskokwim.

The young folks were sick at heart. What is more, neither of the men had ever built anything, and winter was not far away. Mrs. Weinland remembered that her father always nailed outside siding to the uprights at a forty-five degree angle, inside boards at right angles to the outside boards; no wind, he had often said, could blow down a house built that way. Soon the men were hard at work and natives came to watch the strange doings. Weinland thought he might learn a few Eskimo words, so he held up a piece of building paper with a "what is this?" expression. "Nathlorka," said a native. The missionary was delighted; he showed the natives how to nail "nathlorka" to the boards to keep out the wind. They did not seem to understand. In time the missionary discovered that "nathlorka" means "I do not know." Learning Eskimo had its difficulties.

Snow was falling before the missionaries could move into their house. It grew colder and colder, and the long dark days seemed endless. The missionaries had contracted with the government to make daily weather observations at 7:00 p.m. Washington time. Unfortunately that was 1:15 a.m. at Bethel. Gradually they picked up Eskimo words and translated Bible verses into the native tongue. When they held their Easter service at Torgerson's grave in 1888, a few natives joined their circle, and on September 10 eight Eskimos were received as members of the church. In two years the number of communicants increased to more than 200.

The little village of Bethel, in which the work began has now grown into a city of more than 2,000 persons. An American Air Force base has been built about five miles from the town. A Public Health Service hospital supplies medical service for the area. Bethel is also home base for regional offices of the Bureau of Indian Affairs, the Weather Bureau, the National Guard, the Bureau of Fisheries, etc. A new regional high school with dormitory facilities for students from the more than sixty villages of the district makes Bethel an important center.

To meet the challenges posed by these changes, the Moravians some years ago erected a large church building. To adequately serve the high school students coming into the town a Christian education building was erected in 1972, and a second pastor came to live and serve in the town. The buildings of the Children's Home, once so greatly needed, will be converted to other uses. Small pieces of land owned by the church are being sold at modest prices to provide home sites. Thanks to the work of the Rev. Ferdinand Drebert, the entire New Testament has been translated into Eskimo, and is published by the American Bible Society.

The work today is staffed almost completely by native workers with some specialist assistance for theological education. The Alaska church was recognized as a full Unity Province at the 1988 Unity Synod and has assisted with the work of the Labrador Province, the only other Eskimo area of the Moravian Church. Closer relationships between these two areas are anticipated.

The Jerusalem Leper Home (1867)

In 1865 a wealthy German baron named Von Keffenbrink Ascheraden and his wife visited Jerusalem. One day the baroness saw something which touched her heart: a group of lepers, outside a wall, begging money from tourists. Upon inquiry she learned that there was no home or hospital for lepers. No one paid any attention to them unless they came too close. When that happened they were driven away with stones and curses.

Before she returned home, the baroness purchased a piece of ground near the Jaffa gate and arranged to have a small hospital built. When she got home she appealed to the Moravians to provide a staff for the hospital. Her appeal fell upon sympathetic ears, and in 1867 Frederick Tappe and his wife went to Jerusalem to open the Home.

Will There Be Patients?

On the day of dedication there was not a single patient. Fanatical Moslems refused to enter a Christian home; other lepers hesitated to give up their independence. For three months the Tappes waited. Then one poor leper knocked at the gate. By the end of the first year there were twelve patients. Moravians in Germany sent the nurses and deaconesses, and Moravians in England and America contributed to the support of the Home. In 1887 a new and larger home with room for fifty patients was built on the side of the hill.

During World War II the Home experienced hard times. Often medicines failed to arrive, and there was the ever-present danger that Arab and Jewish patients would come to blows. When the Israeli government came into power, the Jewish Medical Relief Organization began to take great interest in the Home and in 1948 they took over the medical work in the institution. (By this time there were scarcely any Arab patients left; the Home had become almost exclusively Jewish.) When the Israeli government offered to purchase the property in 1950, Moravians felt it would probably be unwise to resist. In March 1951 Moravians bid a reluctant farewell to the Jerusalem Leper Home.

But in December 1952 Moravian officials visited Palestine to discover how many lepers there were in Lebanon and Transjordan and to see what was being done for them. When a group of lepers was discovered at Silwan in Transjordan who said, "There are many things we need, but most of all we need someone to care for us," the Moravians sent Sister Johanna, who had been at the Jerusalem Home, and a companion into the area. A wonderful new home was established in Ramallah, on the West Bank, on Star Mountain, near Jerusalem.

The work at Star Mountain underwent major change and was reopened in 1981 as a home for mentally handicapped girls who receive therapy and education in the former leper home buildings. Former leper patients still live in the area and receive some assistance from the staff. Continuing political uncertainties in the area often cause difficulties, but the dedicated staff carries on in the name of the Prince of Peace.

The Support of Missions

The early missionaries of the Moravian Church supported themselves as best they could by working at some trade. On March 30, 1756, for example, missionary Schumann wrote from Surinam, "Brother Kamm is picking coffee; Brother Wenzel is mending shoes; Brother Schmidt is making a dress for a customer; Brother Doerfer is digging the garden; Brother Bambly is working on the canal."

Within a few years, however, it became apparent that while there was no disgrace in any kind of honest work, a missionary could be either a carpenter or a missionary, but he could not be both. Frederick Martin had won a thousand slaves for the kingdom before he died, but he had won them by going day after day from one plantation to another and patiently dealing with every individual. "Is not that the way it ought to be?" people began to ask. "Should not a missionary be permitted to be a missionary?"

So it came about that before many years passed the Moravians in Herrnhut began to take weekly offerings for the support of their missionaries. Baron De Watteville made the first house-to-house collection in 1750. When he knocked at the homes of the poor, he said, "I cannot pass you by because you are poor. Do not give me any money, but bless my collection box." But even the poorest had something to give.

Friends to the Rescue

But even though Moravians learned long ago to contribute to the work of their church, there have been many times when that church could not have survived if it had not been for the many friends God raised up to help. Members of the royal houses of Denmark and Holland gave buildings for the Greenland mission. Wealthy friends paid the passage of many of the early missionaries. By 1755 money was coming regularly from friends in England, Switzerland, Holland, Denmark, and other countries. That support has continued down through the years. In 1896 "a wealthy lady" in England had a prefabricated house and church built in Germany and shipped to Labrador for the new station being established at Makkovik. In 1897 "a friend" paid off the mission deficit of $30,000. In 1913 German Protestants celebrated the silver anniversary of the coronation of William II by raising money for missions. From this effort the Moravian Church received $51,970. In 1927 a conference of Protestant mission societies was held in Herrnhut. By mistake one of the delegates got into the Moravian meeting and heard them discussing the huge deficits they were facing. He went out and appealed to other Protestant groups, saying, "The Moravian Church is not large enough to meet these debts alone. We must all help." This appeal produced no less than $25,000. In 1945 the British Mission Board was "rescued" by the arrival of a registered letter from Denmark containing $50,000. "Our gratitude and our relief," wrote the Mission Secretary, "are both immeasurable." But of greater help than unexpected donations such as these has been the steady help which has come year after year, since 1817, from the London Association in Aid of Moravian Missions. Organized by Anglican friends during the economically difficult days which followed the Napoleonic wars, the Association soon gained support from William Wilberforce, Lady Gladstone, and a host of prominent bishops, clergy, and laypeople. Every year a meeting is held in London at which some famous speaker shares the platform with a Moravian missionary, and there is turned over to the Moravian Church monies (as much as $50,000 at times) which have been contributed by concerned Christian friends in the Anglican and other churches.

The Tailor Shop Has Grown

In 1768 a missionary in Surinam named Kersten opened a tailor shop to support himself and his work. From this humble beginning, what is now the

Moravian Church Foundation has emerged through the years. With a board of twelve directors, the Foundation now contributes heavily to the causes of the worldwide Moravian Church. In the period between 1981 and 1988, almost three million dollars were distributed among thirty-six recipients.

New Look in Missions

What started as a mission work of a European Church has become the ministry of a worldwide fellowship of Moravians who live and work on five continents. Former mission fields now are self-supporting, self-governing provinces of the Moravian Unity and partners with the old sending provinces in the mission of the Church. The many foreign missionaries of a century ago have been replaced with native ministers and teachers, and missionaries now go out from areas which used to receive all of their staff from overseas. The vision of John Valentine Haidt's famous portrayal of the firstfruits of the Gospel gathered around the risen Christ has come to be reality in a church which continues to work to win for the Lamb the rewards of his sufferings.

Chapter 9

The Moravians on the Continent

We turn now from the story of how the early Moravians went out from little Herrnhut into all the world with the gospel to the record of what happened at home while the missionaries were sailing the seven seas.

They Are Not Queer!

It was in 1732 that Dober and Nitschmann set out for the West Indies. For several years before that, Zinzendorf had been worried about what might happen to the Moravians he had befriended. He knew well enough that in many quarters he was considered a heretic who protected strange people who had run away from home. Early in 1729 the count decided to meet some of the opposition head on. He published and circulated a document stating plainly that the Moravians were not members of some strange sect. They belonged, said he, to an ancient and honorable church of which even Luther had approved. There was nothing queer about them.

In January 1732 a royal commission appeared at Herrnhut, remained for several days, asked a lot of questions, and went off. In April the government's decision arrived, "The Moravians may remain; the Schwenkfelder must leave." Soon the Schwenkfelder, whom the count had been sheltering at Berthelsdorf, were on their way to America. They settled in the Perkiomen valley of Pennsylvania, where their descendants live today. Fearing what might come next, Zinzendorf sent a group of Moravians to Georgia, as we have seen. Then the blow fell, not on the Moravians but on Zinzendorf himself. He was ordered to leave the kingdom of Saxony, his home!

Worse Than Greenland!

Zinzendorf wasted no time in crying over his banishment. "What difference does it make?" he asked. "I have no time to stay in Herrnhut anyhow."

But where was he to stay? He soon found an answer. A certain Count Isenberg owned two castles in the Wetterau, outside of Saxony. When he offered to sell them to Zinzendorf, the count sent Christian David to look them over and report.

Christian David came back shaking his head. The castles, he reported, were falling down, the estates were rented out to more than fifty families of tramps and beggars who were at one another's throats. The count was astonished. "Christian!" he shouted. "Haven't you been to Greenland?"

"Yes," replied Christian,"but this is worse than Greenland!"

No doubt Christian David knew well enough how little effect his words would have on the count. Soon groups of Moravians were on their way to the castles in Wetterau. It was 1736. Some of them remained until 1750.

The count had little time to spend with the "pilgrims," as he called them. He made several trips to England, conferred with Archbishop Potter, met the Wesley brothers, and made other contacts. In 1737 he was consecrated a bishop; in 1738 he made his visit to the West Indies; parts of 1741 and 1742 were spent in America. In spite of everything the settlement in the Wetterau prospered. A college was built and schools for boys and girls were opened. Within a few years the schools had 600 pupils, and word had to be sent out that no more pupils could be accepted.

We Choose Christ

During the early days of Herrnhut one of the elders who governed the little community had always been chosen Chief Elder. He had been looked upon as the spiritual leader of the congregation. When the church began growing at home and spreading into lands across the sea, Moravians faced a real question: Shall we now have a Chief Elder for the entire church? If so, will we not soon have a Protestant pope?

The synod of 1741, which met in London, faced this question boldly. "As we began to think about it," Zinzendorf wrote later, "it occurred to us to make the Savior our Chief Elder." The Moravians decided, in other words, that if Christ is really the Head of his church, as they professed to believe, then no human being should ever be chosen "Head" of a church. From that day to this, Moravians have elected persons to be bishops and members of the governing boards, but no one has ever been elected to be "Head" of the church. The date of this historic decision was September 16. This day is still observed as a Memorial Day in our church for the gathering of ministers together for fellowship and rededication.

Strange but Glorious Contradiction

During the last twenty years of his life Zinzendorf ruled the Moravian Church with a firm hand. These years revealed both the strength and the weakness of his character. He was bitterly hated and greatly loved. Twice the king of Saxony banished him, yet King Frederick I of Prussia said, "The Devil himself could not have told me more lies than I have been told about this count. His only sin is that he has devoted himself to spreading the gospel. . .I will do all I can to help him."

No man did so much to keep the Moravian Church from dying; yet this very man's ideas almost destroyed it. Zinzendorf was only twenty-two when Christian David and his friends arrived in Saxony. From that day until he died at the age of sixty, almost every ounce of his strength and every dollar of his money was devoted to the Moravian Church. Yet Zinzendorf's ideas as to what the Moravian Church should be and do kept the church small in Germany, almost killed it entirely in England, and hindered its growth in America. For a hundred years after the death of Zinzendorf the Church grew normally and naturally only on the mission fields.

What was Zinzendorf's idea as to the mission of the Moravian Church? Well, in the first place, the Moravian Church was not to be a church or a denomination at all; it was to be a fellowship of societies of Christians. These societies were not to think about such things as trying to grow or organizing themselves into congregations. They were simply to keep the pure gospel alive in their own groups, preach it to anyone who would listen, be like the leaven Jesus talked about.

No one would deny that this was a noble dream. In Germany it had a fair chance to succeed, for there everybody belonged, theoretically at least to the state (Lutheran) church. In Zinzendorf's day many state church members made light of their membership and scarcely ever went to church. Many of these indifferent members did come, however, to the informal meetings of the Moravian societies, for there was a warmth and friendliness in such groups which they did not find in their church. The result was that Moravian societies sprang up everywhere. Society members read the Moravian Text-book, were visited by Moravian ministers, and gave money to Moravian missions, even though many of them never thought of joining the Moravian Church.

Because the society idea worked well in Germany, Zinzendorf and other leaders who followed him were sure that it was the right plan for every other place. What these good people did not realize was that in England the state church had even less influence than it had in Germany, and that Americans did not know anything about state churches. What is more, the plain truth is that it is hard to keep a plant alive if you deliberately prevent it from putting down roots.

A few years after the Moravians came to England, they had established hundreds of societies in England, Ireland, Scotland, and Wales. If they had organized these societies into congregations, the Moravian Church would be a strong denomination in the British Isles. But because societies were not permitted to develop normally into congregations, the Moravian Church almost died out entirely.

In America the society idea did not have quite so disastrous an effect. In those sailing vessel days America was really far away from Germany, and American Moravians soon learned to stand on their own feet. When they saw that if they wished to survive they must organize congregations rather than societies, they took matters into their own hands and did what seemed best and right.

The Use of the Lot

It was not only the society idea which kept the Moravian Church small; the excessive use of the lot also kept hundreds of potential members out of the church.

Moravians apparently used the lot for the first time when the first ministers of the church were chosen in 1467. The members of synod had spent the night in prayer. When morning came they nominated nine men. Then they took twelve slips of paper. Nine were blank and three were inscribed "Jest" (Bohemian for "this is the one"). The twelve slips were put into a box. A boy was called into the room and asked to draw out one slip for each nominee. Had he drawn out the nine blank slips, no one would have been chosen. It turned out, however, that six men received blank slips and three received inscribed slips. These three were declared "chosen by lot" to be the first ministers of the Brethren's Church.

The early Moravians brought this custom of deciding important matters by appealing to the lot to Herrnhut with them. During Zinzendorf's lifetime the custom came to be used more and more frequently. Usually three slips were placed in a box. One was blank, one marked yes, one marked no. After earnest prayer one slip was drawn out. If the blank slip was drawn, it meant "no decision is to be made now." In such cases another appeal was sometimes made a year later.

In 1769 it was decided that no minister could marry unless his choice was approved by the lot. Later members of the congregations were required to submit to the same rule. No one could join the Moravian Church unless the lot said yes.

The result of this policy was that hundreds of interested people never applied for church membership. To have a "no" slip drawn was a humiliating experience. The whole idea seemed queer to persons who had not been raised on it.

By 1819 the protests of American Moravians had become so loud that synod agreed that church members might marry without an appeal to the lot. Once this break was made, the custom began to pass away, although it was not until 1836 that missionaries were allowed to marry without consulting the lot.

The Death of Zinzendorf

On June 19, 1756, Countess Zinzendorf died. Throughout her married life she had been a most loyal and energetic companion to her husband. After her death the count seemed to lose some of his vast energy and for long periods of time he remained quietly in his rooms at Herrnhut. Again and again he was ill. On May 9, 1760, shortly after having whispered, "I want to go home," he died.

Thus passed from this earth "the patron saint" of the Moravian Church. He was not perfect and not all of his ideas were wise. But in pure devotion to the cause of Christ, and in willingness to carry out the will of God as he saw it, no one shines more brightly.

Will the Moravian Church Die?

"Now that the man who had the money is gone," said Zinzendorf's enemies, "the Moravian Church will not last very long."

Fortunately the Moravians had realized that Zinzendorf would not live forever. In 1755 there had been a conference at which the count's property had been separated from the property of the church and the church property was then put under the care of trustees. It had been decided also that church members should pay dues. They were also to have a voice and a vote in governing the affairs of the church.

These steps had been taken not a moment too soon. After Zinzendorf's death it was found that his properties were heavily mortgaged. Since the Moravians knew well enough that they were the cause of these debts, they offered to buy the Berthelsdorf and Hennersdorf estates from the count's heirs and assume the debts on them. For these properties they paid £25,000 but with them came a debt of £150,000—equivalent in our days, to several million dollars. At the time of the count's death the Moravians had about forty organized congregations in England, Germany and America.

One of the first things they did was to send to America for Spangenberg, the most practical leader they had. In spite of everything he could do, a number of years passed before any impression could be made upon the debt.

"Our Watches and Rings"

In 1772 Herrnhut Moravians celebrated the fiftieth anniversary of the founding of their town. Only one thing, the crushing debt which threatened to destroy their whole church, marred their happiness. In the midst of the celebration the twenty young women who lived in the Sisters' House sent a letter to the governing board. "We have been thinking," they wrote, "about how we might be able with the little we have, to help reduce our church's debt—our debt. We have cheerfully agreed to dispose of our watches, snuff boxes, rings and jewelry of every kind, provided that Moravians everywhere will do the same thing."

This brave letter produced an immediate response. It was circulated among the churches and soon money and gifts began coming from every corner of the little Moravian world. In three years £20,000 had been raised in this way. The castles in the Wetterau were sold; property was sold in England; in America the entire village of Hope, New Jersey, was sold. Little by little the huge debt was reduced. Before many more years had passed, the impossible had been accomplished and Moravians could hold their heads high and thank God.

How the Church Grew in Germany

At the death of Zinzendorf the Moravians had about a dozen congregations in what later became Germany. In the vicinity of Herrnhut were Kleinwelka, Gnadenberg, Gnadenfrei, and several other centers; farther away were Niesky and Berlin. In Holland there was Zeist.

How did Herrnhut develop between 1760 and World War II? When the war began the congregation had more than fifteen hundred members, but this tells only a part of the story. In the early days of Herrnhut the settlers had established stores and mills. These businesses were owned not by individuals, but by the congregation, and the profits they made went to the church. In 1933 there were about sixty business firms connected with the congregation—a bank, hotel, bakery, drug store, stores selling clothing, leather goods, books, imported novelties. In addition to this, the congregation owned many of the buildings in the town, operated several schools, and had homes for the aged. What is more, Herrnhut was the center for "diaspora" work in neighboring communities. Workers went to societies nearby, preached in state churches, circulated Moravian literature, received offerings for Moravian missions. Thousands of people all around Herrnhut knew and welcomed the Moravians to their homes and their churches.

Niesky, which by World War II was as large as Herrnhut, had about the same number of business firms connected with it and operated several schools. Gnadenfrei, with 600 members, had thirty business establishments and four schools.

It was because most of our German congregations were little kingdoms like this that a denomination which had less than ten thousand members in all Germany was able to support several of our largest mission fields and keep perhaps a hundred home missionaries busy in every part of Germany, as well as in Sweden, the Baltic countries, Switzerland, Denmark, and Holland. Many state church members looked upon the Moravians as a kind of interdenominational missionary society and were glad to help them in their work. This help, together with the income from their business establishments, gave the Moravian Church a strength many times as great as its small membership would suggest.

A Moravian Health Center

In 1920 the famous health center at Bad Boll in the Black Forest was given to the Moravian Church. It had been founded years before by Christopher Blumhardt, and upon the death of his son it came into Moravian hands. Today it consists of a sanitorium with sulphur and medicinal baths. Its imposing buildings provide accommodations for several hundred patients, and it is a large and successful Christian health resort.

The Moravians in Holland

In the city of Haarlem there is a little Moravian congregation established in 1744. In Zeist there is a much larger center with extensive and attractive buildings of the old settlement type. Several schools are maintained, and there is a large missionary society to which thousands of state church members belong. Many years ago this society assumed responsibility for the support of Moravian missions in Surinam (then Dutch Guiana). In the city of Amsterdam the coming of Moravians from Surinam has resulted in the organization of a congregation which, in 1970, acquired "splendid new church premises." Continuing immigration of Surinamese Moravians has resulted in more new work and given new impetus to the established centers.

Denmark and Sweden

In Denmark the Moravians have but one congregation, Christiansfeld, founded in 1773. A large church was erected in 1776 and schools, shops, business establishments, and dwellings soon made this settlement a typical Moravian town. In 1843 a missionary association was founded. Through this organization a large group of non-Moravian friends support Moravian mission work in western Tanzania. These friends often use the Moravian Textbook, and often supply nurses and missionaries for the Tanzanian mission. Once every year a mission festival is held at Christiansfeld, and as many as 3,000 persons have come to encourage and assist the Moravians in their work.

In Sweden, Zinzendorf's idea is most completely expressed, for there is not a single Moravian congregation in the country, but Moravians own a hotel and an office building in Stockholm, and several Moravian ministers travel up and down the kingdom visiting societies of Christians who read mission literature and contribute to Moravian mission work.

Poland and the Baltic Countries

Until the Russian annexation of the Baltic countries the Moravians had congregations and societies in these little republics, especially in Latvia. Moravian work in this area goes all the way back to a visit made by Christian David about 1729, and we know that Zinzendorf visited Latvia in 1736. Although Empress Catherine II of Russia, who ascended the throne in 1764, openly encouraged the Moravians, her successors did not feel kindly toward them, and for many years both the government and the Orthodox Church have done everything possible to hinder their work.

In Poland also the Moravian Church has traveled on a thorny path. In 1841 the only Moravian bishop in Poland died. That meant that there was no one to ordain future ministers. The Polish Moravians wrote to King Frederick of Prussia because he was a Protestant and asked if he could help them in any way. He replied, "Choose one of your ministers to be a bishop and send him to Prussia and ask the Moravians in my kingdom to consecrate him a bishop."

The Polish Moravians took this advice and the result was the beginning of a friendship between Polish and German Moravians. In 1925 the Moravians had about seventy centers of work in Poland. The bitterness stirred up by the World Was II and the way in which Poland was finally divided up among its hungry neighbors resulted in complete destruction of the ties between German and Polish Moravians and in the disappearance of most of the Moravian centers in eastern Europe.

Moravians in Switzerland

Moravian work in Switzerland began in 1873. Today there are two congregations (Montmirail and Peseux) and four societies in Basel, Zurich, Berne, and Menziken. Once a year the Moravian mission festival is held here at Montmirail, and to it come friends from all parts of French Switzerland. There is a morning service, French and German meetings during the afternoon, and a closing communion service. Swiss Moravians publish several papers and a French edition of the Textbook.

Moravians in their Homeland

With the story of the persecutions which drove the early Moravians out of Bohemia and Moravia we are familiar. In 1781 the Lutheran and Reformed churches were allowed to begin work in this area, then a part of Austria, but it was not until 1870 that the Austrians were persuaded to grant permission to the Moravians to begin work in the land of their origin. The Austrian government was not very enthusiastic about the Moravians. When the first service was held—at Pottenstein—the minister who was to become pastor of the congregation was required to send cards of invitation to everyone whom he desired to attend. To make sure that these regulations had been complied with, four armed policemen came to the service and made everyone present produce his card of invitation! For ten years local officials put all possible obstacles in the way of the Moravians, but the work grew slowly nevertheless. In 1871 two additional congregations were established, and in 1874 a new building was erected for the orphanage at Rothwasser. Finally in 1880 the Austrian government recognized the Moravian Church.

In 1891 the first congregation in old Moravia itself was organized at Herzogwald, and a few years later the Moravians began preaching at Kunwald, the birthplace of their ancient Unity, and in Jungbunzlau, which centuries before had been one of their strongholds.

The Munich agreement of 1938 sliced off congregations in the Sudetenland, annexing that portion of Czechoslovakia to Germany. Since many members of these congregations had been anti-Nazis, they had to endure suffering under their new government. Bishop Karel Reichel spent three years in a concentration camp, and other ministers and members were mistreated.

In Czechoslovakia, the church continued to grow. Today there are about twenty congregations and the "Jednota Bratrska" sign is found in towns and cities like Prague; Zelezny Brod; Nova Paka, the headquarters of the church; Potstejn, and other towns. The Czech congregations form a province of the Unity. Although historic old buildings such as the magnificent church at Mlada Boleslav were lost to the Moravians centuries ago, the influence of John Hus is still felt not only in our own church but in other Protestant churches as well, for, as an English visitor expressed it, "Although our church is small, it is large in prestige, and enjoys the honor and affection of the modern Protestant community in Czechoslovakia."

Since World War II

When the smoke of World Was II cleared away, the state of the Moravian Church in Germany was pitiful. An early report stated: "Loss in property is almost incalculable...of our church buildings eighteen were destroyed, of our parsonages, twelve. . .of our schools eight were destroyed, six severely damaged. . .of other buildings, seventy-five were destroyed and forty-seven severely damaged." Members were scattered in all directions. When territory along the Oder River went to Poland, for instance, residents of towns like Neusalz were simply driven out to find homes where they could. In 1949, the Neuwied congregation listed 267 "resident" members and 834 "scattered" members; in 1951 more than half of the Moravians in what is now West Germany were still listed as refugees.

Although forty buildings had been destroyed in Herrnhut, services were soon resumed in any available spot. After long delays, the government permitted the rebuilding of the historic Herrnhut church and in other areas permission was given for the rebuilding of some structures, although not always for church purposes.

In Berlin, the buildings of the two congregations were destroyed. One group continued its worship in a barracks building, the other in a small available all-purpose building. Then, in 1960, the two congregations merged and voted to erect a new building. On June 25 the cornerstone was laid with friends coming from many places, and Bishop Otto Dibelius brought greetings from other Protestants. The Berlin brass choir, "a very fine group indeed," played at the service. In East Berlin, Moravian services are held on Sunday afternoons in the lower room of a friendly Catholic church.

In Bad Boll, home of the health center we have described, a congregation was organized in 1945, and this community has become the headquarters of the Moravian Church in Western Europe.

In June 1972 Moravians in Herrnhut celebrated the 250th anniversary of the establishment of the community and official delegates came from many parts of the Moravian world to rejoice with them. In 1977, the John Amos Comenius Retarded Children's Center was opened in Herrnhut, which houses a three-year training program for sixty educable retarded persons.

Here and there new centers of work are arising. In a desolate area of northern Germany lay a prisoner-of-war camp consisting of fifteen barracks. Here groups of Moravian refugees from as far away as Poland began settling in 1945. Within a year's time more than 500 hundred persons called this dreary camp home. With everyone working as hard as he could, the barren ground began to produce food and the buildings were improved and new and better ones added. School was begun in a former stable. On August 13, 1946 a congregation was organized called Neugnadenfeld. There was little in the crude hall in which the worshipers met to remind them of the churches in which they had once worshipped, but the little congregation had six trombones which a woman had saved from destruction and brought with her.

In the little town of Trossen, on the North Sea, a new Moravian School has been opened. At Borstel eight wooden barracks have been turned into a home for the aged. At Wilhelmsdorf in southern Germany, there is a new school for girls; the Koenigsfeld schools have been greatly enlarged. At Zwickau a new congregation has been organized. In 1948 more than a million copies of the Daily Text Book were circulated in Germany, half of them behind the Iron Curtain.

In the old Moravian town of Niesky a Soviet cemetery now occupies the site of the former Moravian Sisters' House. Above the two hundred graves is the Soviet star and the inscription: "You died, that the proletariat might live." But across the square still stands the stone arch of the ruined buildings of the former Moravian School, and carved into the stone above the arch are the words: "I am the Way, and the Truth, and the Life!"

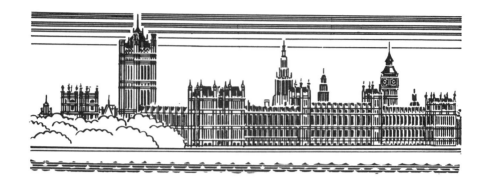

Chapter 10

The Moravians in England

Beginnings in the British Isles

The beginnings of Moravian work in England can be traced to the efforts of Peter Boehler. Boehler, ordained as a Moravian minister in 1737, went to England to arrange for passage to the Moravian settlement in Georgia and while waiting attended the meetings of the Fetter Lane Society. There he was invited to preach and became an influential member of the group. Before he left for Georgia in May of 1738, he had helped John Wesley get peace of mind and had been instrumental in what Wesley always called his conversion. He also had many happy contacts with Charles Wesley.

One of the leaders of the Fetter Lane Society was James Hutton, a Christian bookseller in whose home the group had originally met. Hutton's interest in the Moravians went back to 1735 when he had gone down to the dock to see the good ship *Simmonds* off to Georgia. While bidding farewell to John Wesley, he had met Bishop John Nitschmann and the twenty-three Moravians who were going to Georgia to begin mission work among the Indians. Until Wesley returned in 1738, Hutton received letters from him (parts of his famous *Journal*, no doubt), and in these letters was the story of the Moravians in the storm to which we have already referred.

The Fetter Lane Chapel in time became a Moravian church which served its people until May 11, 1941, when the incendiary bombs of an air raid destroyed it.

The Parting of the Ways

For some months Hutton, the Wesleys, and various Moravians who stopped in London while arranging for passage to America all worshiped together in Fetter Lane chapel. John Wesley became so interested in the Moravians that he even went to Herrnhut "to see the place where the Christians live," as he put it in his *Journal*. There Christian David made a profound impression upon him, and in his *Journal* there is lengthy summary of one of Christian David's sermons and many references to the man.

Soon after Wesley's visit to Herrnhut, trouble began to develop in the Fetter Lane society. James Hutton had always insisted that in his society everyone should be free to speak his mind on any topic which came up for discussion. Now freedom of speech is a grand thing, but it does not always follow, however, that what everybody says is true or helpful to others. Some of the members of the society (like the Wesleys) were highly trained theologians; others had little or no education. Soon some very strange ideas began to be expressed. One young man, for instance, began to assert that since God did everything, those who desired to become Christians should not pray or read the Bible or do anything; they should simply sit back and let God do his work. One day a man named John Bray got up and announced, "It is impossible for anyone to be a true Christian outside of the Moravian Church." Since a careful search of early records indicates that this man never joined the Moravian Church himself, this was, to say the least, a strange statement!

John Wesley was alarmed at this kind of thing. He had been brought up to believe that Christian doctrines were to be accepted, not argued about. When he could not put a stop to all the talking, he lost patience completely and "plainly told our poor, confused, shattered society" that Satan was taking over. On July 20, 1740, he stood up in the meeting, read a statement, and walked out. Eighteen members of the society followed him.

When Zinzendorf was in London a year later, he arranged to meet Wesley, thinking that he might be able to pour oil on the troubled waters. Wesley was not very fond of Zinzendorf, whom he accused of being a dictator. What he did not realize, however, was that it was his own desire to dictate which had led to his break with the society in Fetter Lane. Needless to say, the conference was unsuccessful. Two dictators are not apt to make much progress at a peace conference.

The First Moravian Congregation

After Wesley's withdrawal from the Fetter Lane society the Moravian group became more prominent. James Hutton soon began to publish Moravian literature in English and to sell these books in his shop, The Bible and the Sun. Spangenberg, as wise and great a leader as any group could want, arrived in London. In 1741 he organized a missionary society called the Society for the Furtherance of the Gospel, which is still in existence. Moravians from Germany continued to arrive in London, and by May 1742 twenty men were doing home mission work in and near London. In the fall of that year a group of members of the Fetter Lane society requested Spangenberg to organize them as a Moravian congregation. So it came about that on November 10, 1742, seventy-two persons were organized into the London Moravian congregation. William Holland was appointed minister. James Hutton was the first warden.

Fetter Lane soon became headquarters for Moravian work throughout England. In 1777 the Moravians leased the little chapel for four hundred years and the house at 32 Fetter Lane with it. A passage was made through this house to the chapel and the address of both chapel and house (turned into offices) became 32 Fetter Lane.

Within a short time a number of regular preaching places had been established in London. One of them was in Moorfields where a chapel seating 800 persons was leased. "The London members," wrote Bishop Hasse, "gradually came to regard themselves as a band of workers, ready on the briefest notice to go forth to any part to which they might be sent." The first area in which extensive work was done was Yorkshire, somewhat more than 150 miles north of London.

"Come Over and Help Us"

Up in Yorkshire lived Benjamin Ingham. He had known the Wesleys at Oxford and had gone to America with John. Thus he had met a number of Moravians also. He had completed his education for the ministry but had no church. That fact, however, did not keep him from preaching. Most Yorkshiremen were a rough and ready lot, with little education, and completely untouched by the few churches in the county. Ingham visited the people in their homes, read the Bible to them, and prayed with them. Now and then rowdy mobs stoned him, but he preached on wherever he found a welcome, and his faithfulness soon brought its rewards. In a few years he had organized more than fifty little societies of Christians to which more than 2,000 people belonged. Ingham began to see that unless he could get help his work would gradually fall apart. He thought of the Moravian John Toeltschig, whom he had met when he had been in Herrnhut with John Wesley. He wrote to Zinzendorf, who sent Toeltschig to Yorkshire on a visit. When the people begged Toeltschig to remain, Zinzendorf said, "No." For another year or so Ingham went on as best he could. Then he called a mass meeting of all his societies. "You know what Brother Toeltschig is like," he said. "He is a Moravian. I cannot carry on this work alone. Would you like the Moravians to come and work among you?"

"Yes!" shouted the people.

Once more Ingham wrote to Zinzendorf, who sent the letter to Spangenberg in London. Spangenberg read the letter to the Fetter Lane congregation. Within a few weeks a group of workers was on its way to Yorkshire. When the Moravians arrived a document was actually drawn up and signed by

1,200 people. Benjamin Ingham's societies were handed over to the Moravians.

Zinzendorf in Yorkshire

For some months the Moravians lived at Smith House, a farm near Halifax. They mapped out the entire district and stationed their workers in strategic towns and villages. Within a short time they were preaching in more than seventy places. Just when it seemed as if the Moravian Church was destined to become one of the strong churches of central England, Zinzendorf arrived on the scene.

Zinzendorf had always approved of evangelism, so he was thrilled with the opportunity the Brethren faced. But being a dreamer, he frequently failed to understand plain hard facts, one of which certainly is that if a plant or an organization is to have permanent growth, it must be permitted to put down roots.

Zinzendorf's theories, applied to Yorkshire, meant, "Establish a strong center and concentrate the workers in it; send them out in every direction to preach the gospel." When groups of Christians asked, "Can't we be organized into a Moravian congregation?" Zinzendorf's answer was, "It is not our purpose to organize congregations. Hold meetings in your homes; be a good influence for Christ in your communities and in the state church."

Noble but Not Practical

These were noble words, but they were not practical words. The thousands of persons who had been brought into the light of the gospel by the preaching of Ingham and the Moravians wanted more than informal societies could offer them; they wanted organized congregations which could put down permanent roots in their communities; they wanted real churches. To all of these requests Zinzendorf said, "No."

The Founding of Fulneck

One day in February 1743 Zinzendorf was riding to Pudsey to see the Moravian minister there. On the way he noted a glorious hillside. Immediately he saw in his mind a long row of buildings—a Moravian settlement—crowning the hill and facing the southern sun. He told Ingham about his dream, and a few months later that good man, who was rather well-to-do, had secured possession of the hillside for the Moravians. Word was sent to Moravians in Germany and other places. Hundreds of Yorkshiremen donated their labor and by 1746 the chapel was completed. In 1748 came the minister's house; the Brethren's House (now a part of the Boy's School) and the Sister's House (now a part of the Girl's School) were built in 1752. Within a few years the hillside was crowned with a row of buildings several city blocks in length. Zinzendorf named the settlement Fulneck, in honor of Comenius.

Soon all Moravian activity was concentrated in Fulneck. One business after another was established in the town, so that almost all the needs of the settlers were cared for in their own community. No resident was permitted to spend even a night away from Fulneck without special permission, and none but Moravians were allowed to live in the town. So far did the Brethren go that they required all their members living in other towns to bury their dead at Fulneck. A young Moravian couple living in Mirfield was expelled from the church because in the dead of winter when travel was most difficult, they had buried their child in their own town.

Turned Away

It is easy to understand how the thousands of Christians who had looked forward so eagerly to having the Moravians come to Yorkshire began to lose interest in them. In a few centers, such as Gomersal, Wyke, and Mirfield, the Moravians did build chapels and organize congregations. For the thousands of friends in other societies who repeatedly asked to be organized as Moravian congregations, Zinzendorf finally (1752) issued "A Consolatory Letter," in which he explained why they could not become Moravians. The "consolation" consisted perhaps in the fact that instead of slamming the door in their faces he closed it gently.

Today there are about a thousand Moravians in Yorkshire, organized into about half a dozen congregations in addition to the centers we have mentioned. Crook is up north in County Durham; all the others are clustered around the manufacturing cities of Bradford, Leeds, and Huddersfield. Fulneck, although it has less than 300 members, is the largest congregation in the district.

John Cennick Becomes a Preacher

A Children's Day service in a Moravian Church would scarcely be complete without the singing of John Cennick's hymn, "Children of the Heavenly King."

John Cennick was twenty-one years of age when he became a preacher. He had gone one day to Kingswood Hill, near the city of Bristol, where an open-air service was to be held for coal miners in the area. When the preacher failed to arrive, a number of the miners turned to young Cennick and said, "You preach to us." The young man hesitated, then leaped onto the rude platform. "On the 14th day of June, 1739," he wrote later, "the burden of the Lord came upon me, and I began to open my mouth to testify of Jesus Christ."

For some months Cennick preached up and down the countryside as one of John Wesley's preachers; then he and Wesley parted company. Wesley believed that it was possible for Christians to become perfect. When Cennick refused to accept this theory, Wesley dismissed him. Cennick, however, kept on preaching. Soon he formed a partnership with a Welshman named Howell Harris, and the two men became traveling evangelists. For five years they preached with unflagging zeal. Stones were thrown at them in one village after another; rough men surrounded them and shot off their guns in an attempt to frighten them. More than once they were seized and thrown into the nearest pond. In one village a mob wheeled out the fire engine, filled it with muddy water and played the hose upon them. But Cennick and Harris preached on, and their courage strengthened their converts. By 1743 they had established a center at Tytherton, and societies were springing up in numerous villages around Bath and Bristol. By the end of 1744 the work had grown to such an extent that Cennick decided (as Ingham had done) to ask the Moravians to take over his societies.

Western England and Wales

On December 18, 1745, a group of Moravians arrived in Tytherton to take over Cennick's societies. From the Bristol area the work spread south and west as far as Cornwall and north into Wales, where Moravians were soon preaching in fifty communities but putting down very few roots. As the years passed, traces of Moravian activity in Wales disappeared. In 1957, Haverfordwest congregation, last center in Wales, closed its doors; several years later the old buildings on Moravian Square were torn down to make room for a housing development.

In western England there are ten congregations today. The largest of them is the congregation in Bath. The attractive Moravian church stands upon a hillside on Coronation Avenue. Most of the other congregations cluster around the ancient city of Bristol. In June 1953 the Moravians opened a new chapel in a suburb of Bath. Since it was the first new (Moravian) congregation in England in thirty years, its beginning brought great joy and encouragement to English Moravians.

The Moravians in Scotland

Although individual Moravians had visited Scotland as early as 1743, the first permanent settlement was made in 1763. At that time John Caldwell, an Irishman who had been converted by John Cennick, established a work in Ayr. Caldwell's efforts were most successful, and within a short time he was preaching to crowds of hearers in Edinburgh, Dumfries, Glasgow, and at least twenty smaller towns and villages. But here, too, the hesitancy about establishing congregations led to a gradual collapse of the work. For about 150 years the little congregation in Ayr survived, then that too passed away.

Today only the little Moravian burying ground in Mill Street remains to tell of what might have been.

The Moravians in Ireland

As soon as Cennick had turned over his societies to the Moravians he went to Germany in order to become better acquainted with the Moravian Church. In the spring of 1746 he joined the church he had already served so well. While still in Germany he received an invitation from several prominent Irishmen inviting him to come to Dublin. He immediately sailed for the Emerald Isle.

Upon his arrival he began holding services in a Baptist hall in Dublin, and at the very first service people were turned away by the hundreds. Catholics attended his services in large numbers, and many priests openly endorsed his work. "If you stay in this town," one priest wrote him, "you will make as many converts as St. Francis Xavier." In order to enable more people to hear him, the windows of the hall were removed so that the preacher's voice might travel to the crowds in the streets around the building.

Then, in August 1747, John Wesley arrived. During the years which had passed since his break with the Moravians he had become more and more bitter toward them. A few Moravians had unfortunately responded in the same spirit. When Wesley saw the impression Cennick was making upon Dublin and learned that he had "gone completely over to the Moravians," he resolved to strike a mighty blow. He bought the Baptist hall and ordered Cennick and his friends to vacate it at once. The sudden loss of their building was a serious thing; months passed before they could rent another hall. Although they now organized a congregation, much of the original enthusiasm and interest had spent itself.

Cennick was soon on the move again and for five years he traveled up and down Ireland. His work grew by leaps and bounds. Old records indicate that at one time Cennick and the dozen or more Moravians who came to help him preached in more than 200 communities. Dozens of societies were organized, but once again, scarcely any roots were put down.

Because he cried out once in a sermon that the only God he knew or needed was the Babe in swaddling clothes, Cennick was soon nicknamed "Swaddling John." "There goes Swaddling John," the peasants cried to one another as the preacher's horse went galloping down the road. But even though they made up comic songs about Swaddling John and sang them everywhere, they loved him with all their hearts; and whenever a mob attempted to break up one of his meetings, Swaddling John's friends gave them more of a fight than they had bargained for. Even the penance the priests in County Tyrone imposed upon all who went to hear him preach ("two days' fast and three baths per week") failed to deter the Catholics who flocked to his meetings.

When he was only thirty-six years old his work was done. Riding down from Holyhead to London one day he became ill. He managed to drag himself to Fetter Lane, where friends prepared a bed for him in the chapel. After a few days of high fever and delirium, during which he prayed again and again for Ireland, the flaming spirit of the man who wrote,

Death now no more I dread,
But cheerful close mine eyes;
Death is a sleep, the grave a bed;
With Jesus I shall rise,

went to be with the Lord in whose service he had burned out his life.

Little remains today of the great work he began. Several things explain the collapse of the Moravian empire so nobly built. The first is Cennick's early death. So large a part of the work had been begun and carried forward by this one man, and in the hearts of thousands of Irishmen no one could quite take the place of Swaddling John. The second reason for the decline of the work was the Zinzendorf system of centralizing everything around one main settlement; in northern Ireland it was Gracehill. From Gracehill workers went out in every direction, but only in a very few cases did they actually organize congregations. The third cause of the decline was emigration. The Irish peasants were desperately poor; famine and poverty drove thousands of them to other lands. It has been estimated that during the century between 1750 and 1850 one-half of the total population emigrated. One society after another died because most of its members left the homeland.

Today there are six Moravian congregations in Ireland. Four of them go back to the days of John Cennick: Gracehill with its old, typically Moravian, buildings facing a square; Balinderry, Kilwarlin and Dublin, in Eire. In Belfast there are two churches, of more recent origin: University Road's tall stone church and Cliftonville's attractive brick building. All of the congregations are small. Occasionally attempts have been made "to break through with new work on new estates," but the strength of large denominations frequently overwhelms Moravian efforts, so Irish Moravians concentrate on demonstrating their faith within the limits imposed upon them.

The Moravians in Lancashire

In western England, above Wales, there is a small group of congregations. In 1755 a society of Christians in Dukinfield was organized as a Moravian congregation. Here a new church building was erected in 1970. Not far away is Fairfield, a settlement in the suburbs of Manchester with an imposing array of Georgian brick buildings originally intended to be the center of a district. For many years students for the ministry were trained here. Also in the Manchester area is the Wheler Street congregation. In the cotton-manufacturing city of Oldham are the Salem and Westwood congregations. At Salem, the older town of the two, an old church building had to be taken down in 1960. The congregation then moved into its modern Sunday school building while the building of a new church was undertaken.

Eastern England

The first congregation in eastern England was Fetter Lane in London. As the great city of London grew, the section in which this little chapel stood became a business area. In time regular Sunday services were discontinued, and occasional services were held for the few members who were able to attend. After the destruction of this area of London in 1941, it gradually became apparent that in the rebuilding of the city this area would become exclusively a business section. The Fetter Lane congregation, therefore, transferred its war damage compensation to Upton Manor Moravian Church in East London. Upton Manor's church had been badly damaged. With Fetter Lane's kind assistance Upton Manor was able to repair its church building for its growing youth work and build a new church, rather modern in style, with what the British call "show cases and wide windows under the arcades." In London we also have the Hornsey church, with its beautiful building on Priory Road.

In the city of Bedford, where the Moravians once served a group of societies, there remain today the Queen's Park and the St. Peter's Street congregations. Not far from Bedford are Pertonhall, Kimbolton, and Risley. Near Rugby are Priors Marston and Woodford. Near Derby is the old settlement congregation of Ockbrook with its 200-year-old church and its typical Moravian buildings.

Firm Friends Again

To this rapid survey of Moravianism in England several things should be added.

It is a joy to record, first of all, that in course of time Wesley and the Moravians became friends again. On December 21, 1771, Wesley wrote in his *Journal*: "I met an old friend, James Hutton, whom I had not seen for five and twenty years. I felt this made no difference; my heart was quite open again. . .his seemed to be the same; and we conversed just as we did in 1738, when we met in Fetter Lane." Obviously both Wesley and the Moravians were happy that the old bitterness had been healed. Wesley hunted up the Moravian Bishop Gambold in London and renewed that friendship. When the Moravians were attacked in a popular book by Lord Lyttelton, Wesley said openly that the author did not know what he was talking about. At the age of eighty Wesley went over to Holland to visit the Moravians at Zeist. There he attended the Children's Lovefeast and because it happened on his birthday the children sang their birthday hymn in his honor. The friendship thus renewed the Methodists and the Moravians have happily continued to this day.

The Church Finds Its Mission

At the death of Zinzendorf the Moravian Church had left, out of the hundreds of societies which had once been under its care, about twenty congregations plus twenty-five or thirty societies and preaching places. In strict accordance with Zinzendorf's policy, no attempt was made to organize either the societies or the preaching places into congregations. As a consequence, scarcely a year passed without the loss of a society or preaching place, and the Moravian Church grew smaller every year. About 1800 signs of an overdue rebellion began to appear. In 1806 a chapel was built in the village of Priors Marston and in 1808 a congregation (not a society) was founded at Baildon in Yorkshire. During the next thirty years half a dozen new congregations were organized, but former societies were dying so rapidly that the church continued to decline in size in spite of the new efforts. It was not until about 1850, almost a century after Zinzendorf's death, that English Moravians shook themselves entirely free of the system which had almost wiped their church off the map. Baltonsborough congregation was established in 1859. Before the century closed, thirteen new congregations had been established, and the Moravian Church had begun to take her place as a denomination.

Looking Ahead

There are now about forty congregations in England and Ireland. Many of them are quite small, and only provincial subsidies and local loyalty enable them to survive. The total number of Moravians in the British Isles in only slightly above five thousand. Can so small a denomination survive? Most English Moravians would probably endorse the answer of a delegate to a recent synod, who reported: "It soon became evident that ours is still a church with a mission, actively engaged in the proclamation of the gospel at home and abroad."

What is the situation in the British Moravian Church today? The Moravian schools at Fulneck and Ockbrook are striving to maintain their high standards and continue to influence hundreds of young people, some of whose parents had never heard of the Moravian Church until they enrolled their children. There is a shortage of ministers. However, women are now ordained in this province, and a supplemental ministry on the part of persons who retain their other employment has been implemented.

Early in the 1960s hundreds of Moravians from the West Indies began arriving in England in search of employment. Many of them searched for a long time before finding a Moravian church, but before long their church began looking for them. In 1962, the Rev. J. Kirby Spencer was appointed part-time (full-time in 1964) minister to overseas Moravians. By the summer of 1966 societies of Moravians had been gathered in the London, Birmingham, and Leicester areas (and more recently in Leeds and Manchester areas). On November 2, 1968, a congregation with more than a hundred members was organized in Birmingham, in the presence of over 500 happy visitors. In 1969 a manse was purchased for the minister. On Palm Sunday 1968 nineteen persons were confirmed in Leicester; the society thus begun is cared for by the Ockbrook minister. Hornsey church has a group of overseas members, and cares for the Stoke Newington Society; a society at Brixton is affiliated with the Fetter Lane congregation.

In several areas cooperative efforts have been undertaken. In London, Upton Manor Moravian and Harold Road Methodist churches have united their work. In similar fashion Brockweir Moravians work with the Baptists, and Bedford Moravians with the Presbyterians.

After World War II, when the Fetter Lane area was no longer available for a headquarters building, houses were purchased at 5 and 7 Muswell Hill, London. In these buildings a chapel, offices, a library, and mission apartment constitute the center from which the work of the church in the British Isles is administered.

Chapter 11

The North American Pioneers

On April 25, 1740, George Whitefield and the members of the Georgia Moravian colony whom he had offered to bring to Pennsylvania arrived in Philadelphia. They were disappointed when they found that Spangenberg, whom they had expected to find in Pennsylvania, had returned to Europe, but they felt better when they heard that Bishop John Nitschmann and a group of Moravians had been authorized to come to Pennsylvania to establish a colony. When Whitefield announced that he had purchased five thousand acres of land in the forks of the Delaware and would give them employment at erecting the school he was planning to open for Negro children, the Moravians gladly made the three days' journey through "the northern forest wilds of Pennsylvania" and arrived on May 30 at the place Whitefield had named Nazareth.

For several months the Moravians were busy and happy. Then their leader, Peter Boehler, went to Philadelphia to report to Whitefield. There he was drawn into a theological argument with the evangelist. Whitefield believed in strict predestination and when Boehler said, "Christ died for *all* men," Whitefield ordered him to leave Nazareth and take his Moravians with him. Fortunately, the Moravians had already made a number of friends in the community, and one of them pleaded with the evangelist not to turn the Moravians out during the winter. A few days later Whitefield sent word that they might remain until spring. On December 18 Bishop Nitschmann and his colony arrived in America. Soon they purchased five hundred acres of land about ten miles from Nazareth, at the junction of the Lehigh River and the Monocacy Creek. The Nazareth Moravians decided to move to this new settlement at once. By the end of February the first house on the site of what was to become Bethlehem was completed.

The Moravians had scarcely left Nazareth when an unexpected thing happened. Whitefield's business manager died, and the evangelist found his affairs so involved that he offered to sell his Nazareth holdings. The Moravians in England heard about this and promptly bought the land. By the time this news reached America, however, the building of Bethlehem was well under way.

The Naming of Bethlehem

On November 30, 1741, Zinzendorf arrived in New York. He and his companions were taken to Staten Island, where they spent the night in the home (still standing in New Dorp) of Jacques Cortelyou. Soon the count was en route to Philadelphia. After a brief stay there he set out for the new settlement on the Lehigh River in order to spend Christmas with the colonists. On Christmas Eve there was a celebration of the holy communion. John Martin Mack tells what happened: "The place having as yet no name, it so happened, that on Christmas Eve we called to mind the birth of our Savior, and as there was a thin partition wall between our dwelling and the cow and horse stable, the count in the tenth hour of the night went over to the stable and commenced to sing with great fervency of spirit,

> Not Jerusalem—
> No, from Bethlehem
> We receive life and salvation,

and thus on Christmas Eve 1741 this new settlement received the name of 'Bethlehem.'"

The Count in Philadelphia

On New Year's Eve the count was in Germantown (now part of Philadelphia), where he preached a sermon in the little Reformed church on the square (a bronze tablet marks the spot today). On January 1, 1742, he attended the opening meeting of the first "Pennsylvania Synod." This synod had been called by "Henry Antes and some other Lovers of Peace," as the minutes, printed by Benjamin Franklin, express it, in an attempt to establish friendly relationships between the dozens of sects which were striving to gain a foothold in the little colony. Although Zinzendorf threw all of his vast energy into the project, it was not long before one group after another withdrew, and by 1746 none but Moravians appeared at the meetings of the synod.

In February 1742 the little Lutheran congregation in Philadelphia invited Zinzendorf to become its pastor. After some time he agreed, with the understanding that when he was away from the city a Moravian minister, John Pyrlaeus, should preach in his place.

It became apparent that although many of the leaders of the various sects in the city hated one another, quite a few of them agreed on one thing: Zinzendorf must be driven out of Philadelphia. On the Sunday they selected for this project Zinzendorf happened to be on a missionary journey into the Indian country, so the blow fell upon Pyrlaeus. He tells the story in his journal: "On Sunday July 29 when the gospel was `Jesus wept o'er the city' before the sermon was started, a mob. . .some drunk, dragged me out of the pulpit with much clamor and profanity. The Lutherans and some other devout people having gathered around me in the street. . .now went to my lodgings, where I delivered the sermon. On September 10 the cornerstone of a chapel was laid, and on November 25 it was consecrated."

The chapel to which Pyrlaeus referred had apparently been paid for by Zinzendorf, and in it Zinzendorf organized "an English congregation" on January 1, 1743. Most of the members were Moravians who had recently arrived from England. About this time Henry Muhlenberg, the Lutheran leader, arrived in Philadelphia, and the Lutheran members of the congregation withdrew to establish a Lutheran church. The result was that the little chapel on Race Street became the home of Philadelphia's First Moravian Church.

The Sea Congregations

On the evening of February 26, 1742, 250 persons crowded into Fetter Lane Chapel to bid farewell to fifty-six Moravians who were about to leave London on the long journey to Pennsylvania.

John Philipp Meurer kept a diary of the journey of which the manuscript is still preserved in the Moravian Archives at Bethlehem. On May 1 the voyagers were terrified to note the approach of a Spanish privateer. As their little *Catherine* had no arms, escape was out of the question. The women were ordered below decks to pray. All the men were ordered to take stands around the masts so that the sails could be lowered and the vessel surrendered without loss of life if the Spaniards fired the warning cannon ball. Straight ahead the captain sailed with as steady a hand as possible. Soon the vessels were so near each other that "everything that was taking place on the one could be seen from the other." The Moravians prayed. The Spaniards looked puzzled, but no one moved toward the cannon. After a few moments of suspense the Moravians realized that the privateer was pulling away from them. Soon the dreadful experience was but an unpleasant memory, and

Meurer wrote in his diary, "The Savior's eyes watched over us."

On May 23 the little vessel put in at New London, Connecticut, and everyone had a chance to go ashore. Peter Boehler preached to a curious crowd in the street, and Meurer observed in his diary, "The people called us into their houses and loved us much." On June 7 the vessel reached Philadelphia; the next day the Moravians took the oath of allegiance. On June 18 they set out on foot for Bethlehem. Long confinement on the tiny ship had made some of them almost unable to walk, but they covered the fifty miles in three and a half days. The daily text on the day of their arrival must have seemed most appropriate, "This is the day the Lord hath made; we will rejoice and be glad in it" (Psalm 118:24).

A second sea congregation of 120 persons arrived in December 1743 on *The Little Strength*. In May 1749 the New York *Gazette* reported, "We hear that the snow *Irene*, Capt. Garrison, is arrived at Sandy Hook, from London, with upwards of one hundred passengers on board of the Moravian Brethren."

Indian Missions Begin

While the Moravians were working on George Whitefield's building in Nazareth, Christian Henry Rauch arrived in New York to begin missionary work among the Indians. When he met two Mohicans, Tschoop and Shabash, in the city, he determined to follow them to their homes. Years later Tschoop told what happened:

Once a preacher came and told us there is a God.

We answered, "Do you think we do not know that? Go back home!"

Then another came and said, "You must not steal, nor lie, nor get drunk."

We answered: "Do you think we do not know that? Your people are worse than ours!" So we dismissed him.

After some time Brother Rauch came into my hut and sat down by me. He spoke nearly as follows: "I come to you in the name of the Lord of heaven and earth. He sends me to tell you that he will make you happy and deliver you from your misery. To do this he became a man and gave his life for your sins!"

When he had finished talking he lay down and fell asleep. I thought, "What kind of man is this? There he sleeps. I could kill him. Who would know if I did? He is not afraid!" I could not forget his words. Even when I was asleep I dreamt of the Son of God who shed his blood for me. I told the preacher's words to the other Indians and many came to love the Savior.

An Indian congregation was organized in 1741. In 1742 Zinzendorf made three journeys into the Indian country beyond the Blue Mountains, and at Heidelberg, Pennsylvania, he and representatives of the Six Nations signed a treaty of friendship which provided a welcome for Moravian missionaries throughout the Iroquois lands.

David Zeisberger

For sixty-three years David Zeisberger, greatest of the Moravian missionaries among the Indians, labored faithfully among his adopted brethren and sisters. He began his work among the Mohawks in 1745, but that work ended abruptly when suspicious officials in Albany arrested him as a spy and sent down to the prison in New York. In that city at least a few people knew about the Moravians, so he was soon out of jail and back at his work. For ten years he worked in New York state; then the French and Indian War began. French priests appeared everywhere among the Indians. Jesus, they told the Indians, had really been a Frenchman, born in Paris. The wicked English had put him to death upon a cross. The result of this propaganda was all the French could have hoped for. Soon bands of Indians were scalping every settler they could lay their hands upon. The terror spread into Pennsylvania, and the Moravians in Bethlehem sent a urgent message to Zeisberger, "Come and talk to the Indians; they are killing settlers everywhere!"

The missionary hurried to Pennsylvania; he had contacted only a few tribes when tragedy struck the missionaries at Gnadenhuetten on the Mahony River.

On the evening of November 25, 1755, one of the missionaries heard a noise. He lit his lantern and went out to see if the church door had blown open. He had just left when there was a pounding at the door. Martin Nitschmann opened the door. A crowd of wild Indians gave a war whoop and shot him down. Over his fallen body they fired into the house. Five persons fell dead. By this time the rest climbed into the garret. Only for a few moments were they safe. The Indians set the building on fire. Three of the missionaries jumped from a garret window. Two escaped but the third was caught and scalped. Five persons burned to death in the garret.

The missionaries who had escaped and the Christian Indians in the community fled to Bethlehem. Although the Moravians considered themselves pacifists, they surrounded the town with a stockade and sent to New York for guns and ammunition. For several years Bethlehem was a city of refuge for settlers and Christian Indians from far and wide. When Benjamin Franklin arrived in Bethlehem on an inspection tour of frontier forts, he reported that the Moravians "had even placed quantities of small paving stones between the windows of their high stone houses for their women to throw down upon the heads of any Indians that should attempt to force into them."

The Tuscarawas Valley

On May 3, 1772 twenty-eight Indians began building a village at a place they named Schoenbrunn (Beautiful Spring) in the Tuscarawas valley of Ohio. There Zeisberger and his Indian friend Glikikhan had found a spot where they felt they would be untouched by the Indian wars in Pennsylvania and New York. In August about 200 Indians arrived under the leadership of John Heckewelder and John Ettwein.

Some years ago the state of Ohio restored the village the Indians built so long ago. Today thousands of persons come every year to see the log chapel, the schoolhouse (the first in Ohio) in which more than a hundred Indian children were being taught when the Revolutionary War began, and the cabins of the missionaries and the Indian families.

When the Revolutionary War broke out, British leaders hit upon a novel idea. It was to crush the rebellious Americans between the "redcoats" in the East and the "redskins" in the West! British agents were sent into the Indian country to inflame the Indians against the settlers. This plan failed only because Zeisberger and the Moravian missionaries managed to keep the Delawares and their allied tribes neutral. In time the American government, as we shall see, recognized this important service to our nation.

Tragedy at Gnadenhuetten

In the spring of 1782 Shawnee Indians made several raids upon isolated settlers' homes in western Pennsylvania. During one of these raids they kidnapped a settler named Carpenter. He escaped and came home saying that his kidnappers had spoken German (this is possible, of course, but there is some question as to whether Carpenter knew enough German to be able to distinguish it from the various Indian dialects). However, when Carpenter said "German," numerous settlers who had long resented Moravian friendship with the Indians saw their chance. Soon 150 men under a Colonel Williamson were on their way to the Tuscarawas valley.

When they arrived at Gnadenhuetten, a few miles below Schoenbrunn, they herded all the Indians they could find into two mission buildings. While the Indians sang their hymns and prayed, armed men unworthy of the uniform they wore took them out two by two and killed and scalped them. For several hours the massacre went on and when at last the evil deed was done, ninety Christian Indians had perished. No one has ever been able to find one shred of evidence to connect even one of the Moravian Indians with the raids in Pennsylvania, or elsewhere, for that matter. Today a tall monument marks the spot. Upon its base are the words, "Here triumphed in death ninety Christian Indians, March 8, 1782."

For fifteen years Zeisberger and his heartbroken Indians wandered from place to place. At Mount Clemens they built the first Protestant church in the state of Michigan, and in 1792 they established Fairfield on the Thames River in Canada. Then in 1796 the American Congress, in appreciation of the loyalty of the Moravian Indians during the Revolution, gave the Moravians three tracts of four thousand acres each in the Tuscarawas valley. In the spring of 1798 Zeisberger and a group of Indians came from Canada to build Goshen on this land.

Liquor was forbidden in the little town, but traders in the area got around the prohibition by following the Indians whenever they worked outside the village, treating them to "firewater," and trapping them into crooked bargains of every kind. When the missionaries tried to fight this kind of thing, the traders went up and down the valley urging the Indians to "fight for their rights!" Soon the work of the mission was almost destroyed, and when Zeisberger died on November 17, 1808, at the age of eighty-seven, only twenty faithful Indians remained to weep for their "aged father" and to lay his body to rest in the tiny cemetery. There friends go today to stand at the grave of "the apostle to the Delawares."

In 1862 the Philadelphia artist C. Schuessele painted the well known *Power of the Gospel*, often called *Zeisberger Preaching to the Indians*. In the Moravian Archives building in Bethlehem the painting occupies a position of prominence. No one can look at it without feeling his or her heart strangely touched.

Early Days in the Lehigh Valley

On June 25, 1742, the eighty Moravians who lived in Bethlehem were organized into a congregation. The little community grew rapidly and industry of every kind flourished. Moravian hats and Moravian needlework became famous throughout the colonies. With the proceeds of their industries the residents not only supported themselves but also the many home missionaries they sent into the New England states and down into Maryland.

In June 1742 the school for girls which had been established in Germantown was removed to Bethlehem. By Revolutionary War times Moravian Seminary students included relatives of General Washington, Thomas Jefferson, Nathaniel Greene, and other colonial heroes. In 1746 a "school for bad boys" was opened (first "reform school" in America).

In August 1743 a group of Moravians returned to Nazareth to complete the Whitefield House for new settlers due to arrive from Europe. In January 1744 thirty couples (all had been married in one great ceremony just before leaving Europe) moved into the building. Nazareth soon hummed with activity; the men were busy at farming and the women at spinning and weaving. In 1759 Nazareth Hall, a school for boys, began its sessions in the large stone building originally intended as a manor house for Zinzendorf. In 1763 a printing press was set up at Nazareth. The first book printed was the Passion Week Manual, in the language of the Delaware Indians.

Shortly after Bethlehem was established a few Moravians moved into the vicinity of the present town of Emmaus. When their number had increased to more then forty, they were invited, on July 30, 1747, to come to Bethlehem to be organized into a congregation. The actual organization took place at a lovefeast held at noon. At six in the evening the Bethlehem congregation gathered. The Emmaus group was placed in the middle of the chapel and the

Bethlehem members sat all around them. The Emmaus officers were then installed and everyone joined in a celebration of the holy communion. Then the Emmaus members "returned through the woods."

Central Pennsylvania

On December 2, 1742, Zinzendorf preached at the home of Jacob Huber, near the present town of Lititz; on the next day he preached at the courthouse in Lancaster. Among those present at the Lancaster service was John George Klein. So permanent an impression did the count's sermon make upon him that he gave land, in 1744, for the erection of a church. When a congregation was organized in September 1749, Klein and his wife became charter members. In 1755 they gave their entire farm to the Moravians, and on this property the building of what became the town of Lititz was begun. Soon Lititz became a settlement congregation after the pattern of Bethlehem and Nazareth. Moravians traveling between Bethlehem and Salem in North Carolina were happy to interrupt their journey and spend a night in the neat little town.

Early in 1743 Jacob Lischy settled in Lancaster, in response to the request for a minister which had been made by the Moravians living in the town. In 1746 a church was erected at Orange and Market streets, and in 1749 the undenominational congregation which had been meeting in this building requested organization into a Moravian congregation. Jacob Lischy soon extended his labors to the town of York, and by 1752 a congregation was organized there. The cornerstone of the little congregation's first building was laid on April 24, 1755.

In 1749 a congregation was organized at Hebron, near the present city of Lebanon. During the Revolutionary War the Hebron building was used as a prison for captured Hessians. When the Lebanon congregation was organized in 1848 Hebron members were transferred to it.

Throughout most of its history Graceham, organized in 1758 by missionaries from Bethlehem, remained the only Moravian congregation in Maryland. Then, in February 1964 Trinity Church was organized in New Carrollton; on January 1, 1971, St. Paul's Church was organized in Upper Marlboro. Both of these congregations are in suburban Washington, D.C. Then on May 25, 1986, Faith Moravian Church of the Nation's Capitol was organized, beginning work in the District of Columbia itself.

Beginnings in New York

In January 1741 Thomas Noble, Henry Van Vleck, and a group of Christian businessmen in New York asked Peter Boehler, who was spending a few weeks in the city, to organize them into a Christian society. Boehler did this, and in September 1742 David Bruce was appointed Moravian evangelist for

New York.

Early in 1743 Boehler was back in the city. One evening he was arrested on the charge of having preached in a private home. The mayor ordered him to leave the city. He obeyed and went to the home of Timothy Horsefield on Long Island. There he composed a long Latin document in his defense and sent it to the mayor. Meanwhile some of his friends had taken a different kind of action; they had consulted a lawyer. "According to city ordinance," he told them, "any minister who has been called to be the pastor of twelve or more people is permitted to hold services. There are more than twelve of you. Why don't you call Boehler to be your pastor?" Boehler's friends acted upon this advice, and the preacher came back into the city. Although the Moravians had outwitted their enemies, life was difficult for them for some time. More than one Moravian minister was stoned in the streets. Then something happened in England which helped New York Moravians very greatly.

On February 20, 1749, General Oglethorpe, who had known the Moravians so well in Georgia, offered a resolution in the House of Commons encouraging Moravians to settle in the British colonies. Only one man voted against it. Then, on May 12, Parliament passed an act in which the Moravians were recognized as an ancient Protestant Episcopal Church with doctrines not essentially different from those of the Church of England. Word of the passage of this Act greatly cheered the Moravians in New York, who had in December 1748 organized a congregation. In 1751 two lots were purchased on Fulton Street between William and Nassau, and in June 1752 the little congregation could rejoice in the consecration of its first building. Several trombonists came from Bethlehem to play upon the happy day.

In 1762 Moravians on Staten Island requested that a minister be appointed to reside on the Island. Shortly after that they bought five and a half acres of ground "on the hill" at New Dorp for $124 and began erecting a church-parsonage. The cornerstone was laid in July 1763, and on August 17 the Rev. Hector Gambold and his wife arrived. By the end of November they were able to move into the completed parsonage where they lived for more than twenty years.

Other Pre-Revolutionary War Centers

In 1755 lots were offered for sale in a new community about a mile from Nazareth. In 1762 a church building was erected at Schoeneck (Beautiful Corner), and at a lovefeast held on November 28 of that year the Schoeneck congregation was organized.

In 1768 the Moravians established a settlement congregation at Hope, New Jersey, and built the church and parsonage, a hotel, a mill, and numerous buildings which are still standing. The mill race they cut through a hill of slate rock is still a thing of wonder. Hope flourished for some years, but then Indian raids began to frighten away residents. By 1805 the congregation had declined greatly in size and the school for girls had to be closed. Since the Moravian Church at large was struggling under the huge debts to which we have referred, it was decided to sell the village of Hope, and the final farewell service was held on Easter Day 1808. But in 1946 a plot of ground on Little Silver Lake, near Hope, was purchased as the site for a Moravian camp, and once more, during the summer months at least, Moravians are seen on the streets of the quiet village of Hope.

The Moravians Go South

The passage of the Act of Parliament recognizing the Moravian Church brought the Moravians a great deal of publicity. Soon they received invitations to send colonies to Scotland, Ireland, Nova Scotia, Maryland, and half a dozen other places. When Lord Granville offered to sell then 100,000 acres in North Carolina, they decided to accept his offer. In London plans were drawn for the town which was to be built on the property. It was to have eight streets and the plan showed where the buildings were to be placed. Having done this, it was decided to send Spangenberg to North Carolina to see what land was available.

When Spangenberg and his companions reached Carolina in September, 1752 they hunted up Lord Granville's agent. He had no map of the colony, but he was sure that there were no large tracts of "open" land along the coast. "Then," said Spangenberg, "we shall go west."

The group had scarcely started for the interior when Spangenberg came down with malaria. Feeling that the farther away he got from the coast the better off he would be, he insisted upon pushing on. When he was too sick to ride he would slide off his horse and lie down upon a blanket for awhile. As soon as he felt strength returning the group was on its way again. By the time the little group came upon a vast area of open land in the three forks of Muddy Creek, Spangenberg was quite himself again, and because the countryside reminded him of Wachau estate back in Austria, he christened this new land "Wachau." Settlers later changed the name into "Wachovia."

On August 7, 1753, 98,985 acres of land were conveyed to the Moravian Church. Since the church had little money, "the North Carolina Land and Colony Establishment" was formed. Each settler paid in his money and got his land; in this way the church paid for the tract.

Breakfast at 3 A.M.

On October 8, 1753, fifteen men left Bethlehem bound for Wachovia with all their provisions piled into a wagon drawn by six horses. At night they slept on the ground under the open sky unless it rained, when they permitted themselves the luxury of a tent. Breakfast was at three o'clock; by daybreak they were on their way. When going up hill everybody helped to push the wagon; when going downhill they hung on to the rope which trailed the wagon. On November 17 the travelers reached an abandoned cabin on Moravian land. "We made immediate preparations for the night," says their diary. "Our first service (on Moravian land) was held with rejoicing that our long journey had been accomplished in less than six weeks. Right heartily we sang the stanza composed by Brother Grube:

> We hold arrival lovefeast here,
> In Carolina land;
> A company of Brethren true,
> A little pilgrim band,
> Called by the Lord to be of those
> Who through the world would go,
> To tell of Jesus everywhere,
> And naught but Jesus know!

As accompaniment the wolves howled in the forest near by....The daily text on that day was 'I know where thou dwellest.'"

Soon the little cabin was repaired and additional cabins begun. The first wheat was sown on December 4 and the erection of a mill was undertaken. In 1755 twenty-three single men and seven married couples came from the north. The little village of Bethabara was fortified against Indian attack, and during the local Indian wars often became a place of refuge for scattered settlers. What is more, the only doctor for miles around was at Bethabara.

In 1759 eight married couples volunteered to begin a new settlement three miles away. Since Indians were not kind to new, unguarded settlements, the Moravians rode back and forth between Bethabara and the new town, Bethania, every day. Spangenberg always insisted that no Indian would attack a rider if he rode at full gallop and kept on open land. Each town had its night watchman, and each church had a big bell with a long rope. If the approach of hostile Indians was even suspected the alarm could be given quickly.

"I Will Defend This City"

In 1765 the Moravians began to build Salem, the town which had been mapped out in London years before. Before the first tree was felled a verse was drawn from a box of Scripture texts. It proved to be: "I will defend this city" (Isaiah 37:35). The work had just begun when a group of Moravians arrived from Europe. They had walked all the way from Charleston!

One more congregation, Friedberg in 1772, was organized before the Revolution. Today Carolina's four pre-Revolutionary War congregations all worship in lovely sanctuaries and have attractive Christian education facilities. Bethabara's restored original building is now part of a park and museum area.

Revolutionary War Days

When the Revolutionary War broke out in April 1775, most of the Moravians in America paid little attention to the conflict. Many of them could not understand the anger of their neighbors against the British. They had come to America by way of England, and the British government had been good to them. The Act of Parliament had given them legal standing in the colonies. Governor Oglethorpe and Lord Granville and many other prominent Englishmen had been their firm friends. Then, too, most of the Moravians were newcomers. They had not lived in America long enough to have come to love its "rocks and rills. . .woods and templed hills."

But in December 1776 there occurred an event which was to "Americanize" the Moravians rapidly. On the evening of the third of that month, Drs. Warren and Shippen of the American army arrived in Bethlehem with news to the effect that the general hospital of the Army was to be moved to Bethlehem. Everyone was moved out of the large Brethren's House at once. By next morning wagons bearing sick and wounded soldiers began to arrive. Since no food came for several days, the Moravians brought their own food and fed the wounded as best they could.

For almost a year and a half Bethlehem buildings were "Hospital Zone" for the American army. At one time the little village of perhaps five hundred persons was caring for more than seven hundred sick and wounded soldiers, and at times British prisoners of war were quartered in the town also. During 1777 Lafayette was a patient in Bethlehem. When the dashing young Count Pulaski visited him, the Moravian women presented him with the silk banner Longfellow immortalized in one of his poems.

Throughout these terrible days, John Ettwein acted as chaplain to the sick and wounded troops. Ettwein's nineteen-year-old son volunteered his services as a nurse. In December 1777 malignant fever broke out, and the young man was among the victims.

In March 1778 the hospital was moved to Lititz, where the Brethren's House was already being used as a military hospital. There is no accurate record of the number of soldiers brought to Lititz during the eight months the hospital remained there, but we do know that one hundred and ten soldiers died at Lititz.

Moravian hearts were deeply touched by the sight of so many men suffering and dying for a cause. Long before the war ended writers in the Bethlehem diary began to refer to *"our* army," instead of "the American army" as they had once done. In Philadelphia more and more members of the Moravian Church in Race Street began to take prominent parts in the struggle for freedom. Joseph Dean was a member of the Council of Safety for Pennsylvania, and George Schlosser was a member of the Provincial Council. The first newspaper in America to print the Declaration of Independence in full was the *Staatsbote* published by the Moravian printer Henry Miller. Another active Moravian patriot was Charles Stow. In 1752 he and his partner John Pass had recast what was destined to become the Liberty Bell. George Neisser was chaplain to the Continental Congress while that body met in Yorktown, Pa.

Moravian enthusiasm for America was greatly strengthened also by the many visits statesmen like Henry Laurens, John Hancock, Samuel Adams, Benjamin Franklin, and a host of other colonial leaders made to Bethlehem. Colonial officials published letters in the newspapers expressing appreciation to the Moravians for their many services to the American cause. Benjamin Franklin wrote, for instance, that the Moravians were "a Society I have long esteemed and among whom I have many valuable friends."

But Our Church Wasn't "Free"

The end of the Revolutionary War brought a period of growth and expansion to the new nation. Farther and farther west the pioneers pushed their way; towns sprang up in the wilderness. The circuit-riding preachers followed the people, and most of the Protestant churches grew by leaps and bounds. But the Moravian Church did not grow at all.

When we discover from old records that Moravian "circuit riders" were actually preaching in at least nine of the original thirteen colonies when the war ended, we see readily enough that it was not unwillingness to endure the hardships of pioneer work that kept our church from growing. The reason is seen when we read the instructions J. F. Reichel gave the American Moravians when he visited them in 1779. In language strongly reminiscent of Zinzendorf he announced that work in this country was to be centered around four main settlements: Bethlehem, Nazareth, Lititz and Salem. From these centers Moravians were to go out preaching the gospel wherever groups of listeners could be found. If Christians in preaching places suggested that they be organized into congregations, they were to be told, "Membership in a society does not at all carry with it communicant membership (in the Moravian Church) or preparation for it."

It was the last part of that statement which hurt most of all. Soon many society members began saying, "You needn't bother coming to preach to us. We'll get a minister who will take us into his church too." At the time the bishop visited America, Moravians were preaching regularly to at least twenty-five societies; not one of them, as far as can be discovered, ever became a Moravian congregation.

There Was Some Growth

Although organization of new congregations was practically forbidden, the years following 1776 did see growth in some areas.

Moravian schools prospered, for instance. In 1785 the Seminary for Girls, in Bethlehem, opened its doors to non-Moravians. George Washington visited the school and his grandniece, "the beautiful Eleanor Lee," soon became a pupil. (In 1954 this institution moved to a lovely new country campus at Green Pond, merging with Moravian Preparatory School in the 1970s to become Moravian Academy.)

In Lititz, Linden Hall admitted "little Peggy Marvel" as the first non-Moravian, in 1794. (This institution, now a high school on a campus combining modern buildings with ancient structures, enrolls students from many states and foreign countries.) Nazareth Hall also expanded in early years and prospered during the last century, but increasing debts forced its closing in 1929.

In North Carolina, the Academy for Girls, established in 1772, has grown into an academy and a college, with modern buildings and a wide influence in educational circles.

It was during these years also that American Moravians organized their foreign missionary society. The Society for Propagating the Gospel came into existence on November 1, 1787. After the society had been incorporated, Bishop Ettwein sent a copy of its constitution to General Washington. A friendly reply commended the work of the society. When Washington became president, the directors of the Society for Propagating the Gospel sent him their greetings through the Moravian minister in New York. Shortly thereafter came Washington's reply, ending, "I pray Almighty God to have you always in his holy keeping, G. Washington."

In 1803 the cornerstone of the new church (now Central Church) was laid in Bethlehem. Dedication of the building took place

on May 18, 1806. This building, still an imposing structure, was at the time of its erection the largest church building in all Pennsylvania. It cost more than $50,000, a huge sum of money in those days. Strangers came to stare at the Brethren as they dug out the huge basement and began laying up the foundation walls, six feet thick. The building of a church large enough to seat three times as many people as lived in the entire town was a magnificent achievement. It showed, however, that the Moravians still had the European "parish church" idea. From this great center their home missionaries were to go out into all the countryside.

Big Noise in Nazareth

Although there was outward compliance with the rules laid down by the church in Europe, it became more and more apparent that American Moravians were not going to tolerate these restrictions indefinitely. In North Carolina, for instance, a group of English-speaking settlers asked the Salem Moravians to preach in the schoolhouse they had built about six miles southwest of the town. The Moravians agreed; what is more, they conveniently forgot the rules and organized this group, on August 28, 1780, into Hope congregation, the first English-speaking Moravian church in the South. Friedland, where Moravians from Broadbay, Maine, had established a colony in 1770, was organized in the same year, but that was intended to be a settlement congregation of the approved type.

Up in Pennsylvania dissatisfaction with "old-fashioned ideas" expressed itself in other ways. Early on the morning of July 4, 1787, the peaceful village of Nazareth was startled by the shooting of a cannon. It was soon discovered that some of the young folk had decided to celebrate Independence Day. In spite of a plain lecture upon their scandalous conduct the cannon went off again a year later. These young folk were Americans, and they wanted everybody to know it. In October 1790 quite a few of the Nazareth men walked over to Easton to cast their votes for governor of Pennsylvania.

Moravian College and Theological Seminary

In June 1802 principal Jacob Van Vleck of Nazareth Hall made a startling proposal: "Should we not be able to train ministers in this country? Why must we import all of our ministers from Europe?"

In North Carolina the Rev. Christian Benzien strongly seconded this proposal. "Right now," he said, "we need a missionary for our Cherokee Indian work. Months will pass before a minister can arrive from Europe, and then he will have to learn English. If we could train ministers in this country, perhaps more of our young men would volunteer for preaching or teaching in our schools. At present only a very few can bear the expense of going to Europe for their training."

In April 1805 authorities in Europe agreed to let the Americans see what they could do. On October 2, 1807, a theological seminary was opened in a part of Nazareth Hall. The brethren Ernst Hazelius and John C. Bechler were the first professors. First students were William H. Van Vleck, Peter Wolle, and Samuel Reinke. All three eventually became bishops of the Moravian Church.

Within two years progressive head professor Hazelius, chafing under the strict rules he was compelled to enforce, resigned to become a professor in Hartwick Lutheran Seminary. This was a severe blow, but it did stiffen the determination of many American Moravians to have "home rule." The little seminary survived, moving from Nazareth to Bethlehem. Before long a college was added and another move was made to what was then open land at the edge of the city. More years passed, and the Women's College division of the Seminary for Girls merged with the men's college. Today Moravian College with more than 1,200 students (plus night school and summer school students) enjoys the use of both college campuses, and has an imposing group of completely modern facilities for science, library, physical education, college union, dormitory and other use.

A Preacher and a Storekeeper

Soon after David Zeisberger brought his Indians back to Ohio's Tuscara-was valley, it became apparent that the Indians could not occupy more than a small portion of the 12,000 acres Congress had given the Moravians. When an appeal was made for settlers to go to Ohio to help "hold" this land for the church, eight families volunteered to go, provided the Society for Propagating the Gospel would send a preacher and a storekeeper with them.

The new settlers arrived on May 6, 1799. The Rev. Lewis Huebner had come with them, and David Peter had agreed to open a store for them. On July 6, 1800, the Gnadenhuetten congregation was organized, and in 1803 the first church building was erected. One hundred years later the congregation erected its present beautiful John Heckewelder Memorial Church. A short walk from the church stands the limestone shaft marking the site of the Gnadenhuetten massacre.

In 1810 the Moravian minister began preaching to settlers near the town of Tuscarawas, and on New Year's Day 1815 forty-one persons established the Sharon congregation. The log church Sharon members erected in 1817 gave way in 1857 to the present large building.

Even though these early settlers had been sent to Ohio by the "foreign" missionary society of the denomination to hold Moravian land, their going marked an important break with tradition. They showed that the Moravian Church could and ought to expand.

Chapter 12

Our Growing Church

Carolina Takes the Trail

As news of the Ohio adventure reached various areas of our church in America, Moravians in several of the long-established congregations began to think seriously of "going West," and taking their church with them.

The first group to take the trail came from the Hope, North Carolina, congregation. About 1825 members of this church began moving into the Indiana Territory. Among the first settlers was Martin Hauser, a Sunday school worker and lay preacher. A few years later he and a group of friends sent a letter to the authorities in Bethlehem asking if they would advance the money needed to purchase land for the beginning of a Moravian congregation.

The Provincial Board carefully considered this bold request, and then said, "Yes." With the $200 they gave, a 160-acre farm was purchased where the town of Hope, Indiana, stands today. The erection of a log building was begun on April 5, 1830, and shortly after it had been completed, a congregation, later named Hope, was organized. In 1833 Brother Hauser made a visit to Bethlehem to be ordained. "I was not in circumstances to get a black coat," he wrote in his diary, "so I had to be ordained in my blue coat with metal buttons."

In 1859 the Hope congregation opened a day school which later developed into Hope Seminary for Girls. The Seminary started with about fifty pupils and had ten prosperous years. Then it began to run into debt, and after a valiant struggle, had to be closed in 1881. In 1875 the congregation erected its present building, adding a Sunday school annex in 1951.

Some of the North Carolina Moravians who started for the West did not stop in Indiana, but went on to Illinois. After a time Martin Hauser visited the group living in what later became Edwards County, and here, at a place they later named West Salem, he in 1844 organized a congregation in Peter Hinkle's barn. In 1849 a colony of forty-six Moravians arrived from Germany, so for many years there were two congregations, an English and a German, in the town. In 1915, when language problems no longer existed, the two groups united to form one congregation. The large building of the former German congregation became the home of the united congregation. In the well-kept cemetery (in which Ripley says there is the world's smallest tombstone— seven by ten inches in size) there is an attractive arch erected in memory of Martin Hauser, founder of the congregation and the town.

In 1850 a group of North Carolina Moravians went to Iowa, where they bought land from the Mormons and established a settlement they called Moravia. In course of time the Moravians organized no less than ten congregations in Iowa. Unfortunately most of the new settlers among whom they worked were desperately poor, and the denomination had no home mission funds with which to help struggling congregations. One little congregation after another died. Last to survive was Gracehill, which had to close in April 1970.

Seven Cents per Bushel

In 1852 church extension received another push, this time from Frankfurt, Germany. For some years the Moravians had had a society in that city; now these society members decided to go to America. Someone spoke to them about a place called Watertown, in Wisconsin, and they decided to go to that place.

Passage on a freight sailing vessel was best they could afford, and it was eleven weeks before they landed in America. When at long last they arrived in Milwaukee, they found that Watertown was sixty miles away and that they would have to walk that distance with their possessions following them on ox wagons. South of the little village of Watertown they began felling trees for their houses. In order to obtain a bit of money they carefully burned all the branches and sold the ashes (used for making lye) at seven cents per bushel.

On May 11, 1853, home missionary John G. Kaltenbrunn arrived in Watertown. The little band of Moravians rallied around him, and on June 17 fourteen families were organized as the Ebenezer congregation. For several years a log building served as church, school, and parsonage. In 1856, the congregation erected a substantial brick building.

In the town of Watertown, Kaltenbrunn organized a congregation in 1854. Lake Mills congregation was founded in 1856, Mamre in 1859. Today Watertown and Lake Mills are strong congregations with large and attractive church plants.

Although missionary Kaltenbrunn "retired" when he was seventy-five, he continued to preach throughout the area until he was eighty-eight. Greatly loved and honored, he died in 1895 at the age of ninety.

The Scandinavian Churches

In October 1849 the Moravians commissioned John Frederick Fett to work among unchurched Germans in Milwaukee. Soon after he arrived in what was then a city of about 18,000, he met Andrew Iverson, leader of a little society of Norwegian Christians. Iverson and his friends had been trying to contact the Moravians for some time, and therefore welcomed Fett with open arms. The result of this friendship was that in May 1850 Iverson was ordained and he and his society received into the Moravian Church. In a few months they decided to move northward. They packed their possessions and went to Green Bay; then pushed up the peninsula to a spot they named Ephraim. Here they were reorganized as a Moravian congregation. In 1857 they built their first church, "a commodious log cabin," crowned by a twenty-foot steeple built by Iverson himself. Ephraim is now a popular summer resort, and the little white Moravian church on the hill is filled with visitors every summer. From the humble beginnings at Ephraim the work spread to Sturgeon Bay, and back to Fort Howard (now Green Bay, West Side).

In 1850 Fett organized a congregation among the Germans in East Green Bay. In 1961 this congregation moved into a lovely new building in the Allouez suburb of the city. West Side congregation had erected a modern church plant on Oneida Street in 1958.

Growth in the "Home States"

While the Moravians were pushing westward, a number of new congregations were organized in the East and in the South.

In 1837 a group of Germans in Wayne County, Pennsylvania, organized the Hopedale congregation (usually called Newfoundland from the name of the town). In 1842 Ohio Moravians organized a congregation in the town of Canal Dover (now just Dover). In New York City a second church came into existence in 1852. This church continues its work today in a modern building in the Bronx, as the Tremont Terrace Moravian Church. In 1853 the Brooklyn congregation was organized, and in 1854 a congregation was organized in the city of Utica, New York.

In the South there was some expansion also. In 1839 home mission work was begun in the famous Blue Ridge Mountains of Virginia, where the Mount Bethel congregation was organized in 1852. In 1846 Salem Moravians began preaching in a schoolhouse six miles west of their town. Out of this effort has developed the strong New Philadelphia congregation in what is now a growing suburb of the city of Winston-Salem. About 1850 Olivet was organized as a Sunday school and eventually became a chapel of the Bethania congregation. In 1955, after working together as one congregation for over one hundred years, Bethania and Olivet were divided into two separate churches. Services begun in 1854 in another community west of the Yadkin River led to the organization of Macedonia congregation.

We Want Home Rule!

When American Moravians met in Synod at Bethlehem in 1855 they faced the facts. For at least twenty years they had been making definite efforts to expand their church. They felt that they had been doing the right thing. "The old rules and restrictions," they said, "must be taken off the books. We do not want to cut ourselves off from our brethren in Europe, but we must tell them in kindly but firm fashion that we must be permitted to rule ourselves. We must be allowed to elect our own officials, and our synods must be given power to legislate for us."

As if to help the cause along, Moravian ministers on both sides of the Atlantic began receiving copies of an anonymous booklet, "The Moravian Church: What is the Truth?" The author of this booklet contended that Zinzendorf's "church within a church" idea had outlived its usefulness. Moreover, the author condemned the smugness of Moravian leaders and berated them for their unwillingness to consider new ideas. It turned out in time that the author of the scandalous booklet was actually a German, although he was serving as a missionary in Jamaica. Small wonder that delegates went to Herrnhut in June 1857 feeling that a crisis was approaching.

Synod opened with a memorable sermon by Bishop John Nitschmann on the unity of the Moravian Church throughout the world. This unity, he said, was based upon common faith in and mutual love for Jesus Christ. Under the influence of these words the members of synod began their work. Day after day they studied the demands, proposals, ideas. In the end they wrote a new constitution for their church. It was still to be one church in all the world, but every province was to be free to govern itself in all its own affairs. General synods of the worldwide church would meet from time to time, but they would concern themselves only with matters of doctrine, liturgy, election of bishops. The Americans got what they wanted; but best of all, everybody else went home feeling happy, too.

Land of Laughing Water

In the very year (1855) in which Longfellow wrote his poem about the land "where the Falls of Minnehaha flash and gleam among the oak trees," a little group of Moravians from Newfoundland, Pennsylvania, settled in a spot about thirty miles from the famous falls. In and around the little town of Chaska, Minnesota, they staked out claims. In response to their appeal to the Moravian authorities for a minister, Martin Erdmann of York, Pennsylvania, started for the West, arriving in Chaska on December 17, 1857. Two weeks later twenty-eight persons became members of the Chaska congregation. Within a few months congregations sprang up at Zoar and Lake Auburn. In later years the members of Zoar transferred to the Waconia congregation, established in 1915. In 1864 an Academy was founded in Chaska. It struggled for five years to establish itself; then the building was sold to the town for use as a public school.

Ten years after the beginnings of Chaska the Bethany congregation was organized near the city of Winona, and in 1868 the Hebron congregation was established. These two congregations merged to form Our Saviour's congregation in 1976. A few miles away is the attractive brick church of the Berea congregation. In the college town of Northfield the Moravian congregation, organized in 1869, built a new church building in 1953. Christ's Community Church was begun in Maple Grove, a suburb of Minneapolis, in 1981.

The Moravians in New Jersey

In 1853, home missionary Philip H. Gapp began making periodic visits to Camden, Palmyra, Riverside, Westfield, and other towns, preaching to unchurched German settlers. A congregation near Atlantic City survived only briefly, but the Palmyra congregation, organized in 1863, and Riverside, organized in 1865, have survived. The present church building at Palmyra was erected in 1902; a modern Christian education building in 1960. In Riverside the present stone church was built in 1912 and a Sunday school building erected in 1954.

In 1859 the Moravians began work in Egg Harbor City, at that time a town of 1400 persons, but without a church of any kind. Many of the town's citizens openly opposed the coming of a church, and for many years the congregation had a hard struggle. Today, however, it is well established with attractive church, parish house, and parsonage.

In 1865 New York City ministers preached for the first time in the growing city of Elizabeth, where a congregation was organized in 1866. In 1910 the congregation moved to Reid and Lafayette Streets. As the years passed, it became apparent that growth could not take place in this restricted area; so, when a new congregation was established in 1953 in the Battle Hill area of Union, New Jersey, Moravians in Elizabeth voted to transfer their assets and interest to this new work. A congregation known as Evangel Moravian Church was started at Toms River in 1980 and moved into own building in 1989, making this the fifth congregation in New Jersey.

The Western States Again

In 1867 a group of Moravians from Utica, New York, migrated into the "thumb area" of Michigan. In 1870 they organized the Unionville congregation and erected a church; in recent years they have added an annex. Across Lake Michigan is the Daggett congregation, established in 1911 by Moravians who had sailed across Green Bay from the older congregations in Door County, Wisconsin. In the Westland suburb of Detroit, the first Moravian service was held in September 1958 and its church sanctuary in 1969. Faith Church at nearby Canton was organized in 1981.

About 1870, Minnesota Moravians began moving into the fertile Red River Valley area of North Dakota. In 1878, the Goshen congregation was established about twenty miles west of Fargo. Within a few months the work spread to Canaan. In 1914 this congregation replaced its original building with a handsome brick church. Bethel was organized in 1891 and erected its building ten years later. In the city of Fargo a congregation was established in 1943; its church building was completed in 1951. In recent years, as farms have become larger and larger and rural population has declined, the North Dakota congregations have had to share pastors.

The Moravians in Canada

About 1886 little groups of Moravians began arriving in the wilderness which surrounded the town of Edmonton, Alberta. They were Germans who had gone to the Russian Province of Volhynia to escape the ravages of the

Napoleonic wars. In Russia they had established two congregations, only to discover that Protestants were not liked in Russia. One very popular method employed to discourage Protestants was to draft their men into the army for long periods of service. A few of the Moravians, thoroughly discouraged, forsook everything and migrated to Brazil; others decided to go to western Canada.

When at long last the settlers arrived in their new home, they were penniless. Many of them survived the first bitter winter only because the woods were filled with wild game; rabbit meat was the only meat many of them saw for months. One day a government ranger came upon a settler out hunting. Because he had no license, the ranger, in spite of the settler's plead that he had no money with which to buy one, "let him off easy" by confiscating his rifle! If that settler and his family had not had friends, they would have starved to death.

In 1894 Moravian authorities responded to a request from these Canadian settlers that a minister be sent to them. In May 1895 Bruederheim was organized. A month later Bruederfeld came into existence. Each congregation received a grant of forty acres from the government, and log churches and parsonages were erected in each place. Heimtal was organized in 1896, and work began in the town of Calgary in 1902. Here, in what is now a large city, a second congregation, Christ Church, was organized in 1967, and a lovely building was erected in Willow Park area.

In 1905 work began in Edmonton. This congregation erected an impressive building in 1957. In 1962 the Rio Terrace congregation was established in a growing suburb of the city. Recently Edmonton has incorporated the Bruederfeld church within its city limits, so the congregation has built a new facility and adopted the official name of the area: Millwoods. A new work at Sherwood Park was begun in 1982, and work among West Indian Moravians in the Toronto area was started in 1983. This last work, while in Canada, is part of the Eastern District.

The Canadian District has its own camping facilities for all age groups on Cooking Lake in Alberta's Beaver Hills, called Camp Van Es.

Our Canadian District has had more than its share of difficulties and problems. Crop failures have caused once prosperous communities to decline. In Calgary the Moravians were caught in the collapse of a real estate boom. They sold their little building at a very high price and began the erection of a handsome structure on a hill overlooking the heart of the city. Before more than a fraction of the purchase price had been paid the boom collapsed, leaving the little congregation with nothing but huge debts. It took years of help from the denomination to save the congregation from disaster.

The Canadian District can point with pride, however, to the fact that it has excelled every similar area of our denomination in the proportionate number of sons and daughters it has sent into ministerial or mission service.

Expanding in the Eastern States

When church extension received official blessing in 1857, there were ten congregations in Pennsylvania. The first new church after this date was Canadensis, where the Newfoundland pastor had begun preaching in 1859. In 1955 a new church building was erected.

In Bethlehem a Sunday school organized in 1860 eventually became the West Side Church, which in 1954 rebuilt and enlarged its home. The South Side Church, which grew out of the Sunday school Amanda Jones conducted during Civil War days, sold its property in 1962 and moved to Jacksonville Road under the new name Advent Moravian Church. Near Moravian College is College Hill Church, outgrowth of the Laurel Street chapel begun in 1887. The Sunday school which Moravian Theological Seminary students began in 1918 has become the Edgeboro Moravian Church. The new East Hills congregation completed its sanctuary in 1967. Coopersburg congregation was begun in 1883 by Emmaus pastor; in 1950 the Coopersburg pastor began preaching in Center Valley, and in 1952 a chapel was purchased for this congregation. This congregation opened a new church in 1988. In 1888 services were begun in Easton, and this congregation's imposing structure was erected at 10th and Bushkill Streets in 1929.

Only the devotion of businessman Alexander Renshaw, who served as a pastor without salary, kept Philadelphia's Third Church, organized in 1868, alive for its first decade. The present stone-front building on Kensington Avenue was erected during the fifty-year pastorate of the Rev. F. E. Raub. After First Church was closed in 1965, Redeemer Church was dedicated on November 21 of the same year, in the Eastwick section of Philadelphia.

In the city of York several Sunday schools in which Moravians were active resulted in the organization of Bethany and Olivet congregations. They merged into Covenant Church, and an attractive modern building on Red Lion Road was dedicated on April 23, 1967.

In the city of Allentown, Calvary Church was organized in March 1939, and two years later the first unit of the church building was erected at 21st and Livingston Streets. In 1945 the Midway Manor congregation was organized at the opposite end of Allentown. The building which had been purchased here was soon outgrown, and in 1950 the first unit of a new church plant was erected in this growing community.

During the First World War Moravian work began in Reading, Pennsylvania, and a church, at Locust and Perry Streets, was opened in March 1921. In 1948 services held in a tent in Palmer Township, near Easton, marked the beginning of the present large congregation, housed in a modern church plant. The same year witnessed the beginnings of Mountainview congregation in Hellertown.

In 1882 First Church in Utica, New York, began a Sunday school in a tailor shop in East Utica. This developed into Trinity Church, which worshiped in a building on South Street until 1964, when it merged with First Church. The united congregation then erected a beautiful new building on Higby Road, in the adjoining New Hartford area.

First expansion in New York City after 1857 was on Staten Island, where a chapel was erected in 1873 as a home for the Castleton Hill congregation; the chapel has long since given way to the imposing structure on Victory Boulevard. In 1877 another preaching place was established at what is now called Great Kills. These two congregations have their own ministers and church plants, but legally they constitute, with New Dorp, the United Brethren's Church on Staten Island. This threefold congregation with more than a thousand members owns the beautiful Moravian Cemetery at New Dorp. In Stapleton, Staten Island, there is the Vanderbilt Avenue Church, outgrowth of a Sunday school begun in Rocky Hollow in the 1880s. The small Prince of Peace congregation, formed in 1975 through the merger of the Midland Beach and New Dorp Beach Trinity congregations was closed in 1989.

About 1900, West Indian Moravians began coming to New York City. First Church then sponsored the organization, in 1901, of Third Church. In 1968, Fourth Church, begun by Dr. Charles Martin, a native of Antigua, in 1908, merged with Third Church forming the United Moravian Church. Urban renewal has meant relocation of the United Church in the east Harlem area of metropolitan New York. The John Hus congregation in Brooklyn was organized in 1966. Two newer works among West Indians have been organized in Queens and Brooklyn in the past fifteen years.

Growth in the Middle States

In October 1874 thirty-three persons living in the town of Uhrichsville, Ohio, organized a Moravian congregation. Times were hard, and it took the little group three years to complete the grey sandstone church which still stands near the center of the town.

In 1882 a congregation was begun in Port Washington. In recent years this little congregation shared its minister with the Fry's Valley Church, which goes back to 1857, until Port Washington was closed in 1973.

A second congregation was begun in Dover in 1925 and continued until 1988, when it merged with the Dover First congregation.

In the fall of 1947 Moravian services were begun in New Philadelphia, in Trinity Episcopal Church. This congregation in 1955 erected a new building in the Schoenbrunn area.

In 1984, work was begun in the Dublin suburb of Columbus, Ohio, which was organized as the Redeemer Moravian Church in the next year. The congregation erected its own building in 1989.

First Church, Indianapolis, Indiana, was organized in December, 1894. After losing its first building by fire and moving several times, a new church was erected in the Haverford area of the city in 1949. One of the Sunday schools begun during the Rev. Christian Weber's pastorate led to the organization of Second Church in 1924. In 1967, Bethany congregation was organized in a new building completed by the end of the year.

Development in Wisconsin

The year following the Civil War saw the beginning of a number of congregations in the state of Wisconsin. Freedom was organized in December 1866 as the result of evangelistic services held in the community by the Green Bay minister. In 1885 the Windsor congregation came into existence. When a move was made in 1922 into the town of DeForest, the congregation changed its name accordingly. In 1888, Moravian services began in Grand Rapids and Centralia. These towns eventually became the city of Wisconsin Rapids, and in 1946 the German and Scandinavian congregation merged. In 1958 a new, modern building was erected for this congregation. In 1889, fifteen families organized a congregation in the town of London, and built a church in 1894. In October, 1928, work began in the capital city of Madison. Today two congregations, Glenwood and Lakeview, carry on their work in attractive buildings. In 1932, a little Swedish congregation at Stockholm joined the Moravian Church.

After years of planning, Western District Moravians purchased two hundred acres of land at Mount Morris in east central Wisconsin, and in 1969 the development of Moravian Camp Mount Morris got under way around Little Lake, near Wautoma, Wisconsin. A renewal Center was built at Mount Morris in 1973.

How One Congregation Grew

When Bishop Edward Rondthaler arrived in Salem, North Carolina, in 1877, the Moravians had only the Home Church and the St. Philips mission in the city. For years the South had been going through Reconstruction days and times had been difficult. Growth had been slow. In 1870 Kernersville Moravians had been recognized as a separate congregation, and ten years later Providence congregation had been organized. When a number of Providence members moved too far away to attend their own church, Oak Grove congregation was organized. Thus, during more than twenty-five years, only three new churches had been begun.

Shortly after Bishop Rondthaler's pastorate began, the Moravians in East Winston were organized into Fries Memorial. In 1946 this congregation moved to the western part of Winston-Salem and erected a new church plant. In 1893 Calvary Church grew out of a Sunday school started four years earlier in the neighboring town of Winston. Christ Church was begun in 1893 as a Sunday school in a little building arranged so that it could be converted into a dwelling if the project failed. Encouraged by the way in which the Winston venture turned out, Salem Moravians began another Sunday school in 1895; in 1908 this project became Fairview congregation, now moved to a new location on the west side of Winston-Salem.

Gradually Winston-Salem Moravians became more and more enthusiastic about church extension. In 1912 a new building was erected in the southern part of the city for Trinity Church, which had grown out of work established at Centerville back in 1886. In 1927 the first Christian Education building in the Southern Province was added to Trinity's building. The year 1912 also saw the organization of Immanuel Church. In 1923 Trinity began a Sunday school which eventually grew into the New Eden congregation. Early in 1954 this congregation sold its property to the Western Electric Company to become part of the site of a new plant. The first unit of a new building project for the congregation, located in a nearby residential area, was completed in 1954. Another of Trinity's Sunday schools developed into what is now Pine Chapel. Ardmore, one of the more recent churches of the Salem Congregation, was organized in 1924.

After having worshiped in several buildings St. Philips congregation moved, in 1967, into a purchased building with facilities for the Day Care center operated by the congregation. When the Young Adults of the province purchased land in a new area of Winston-Salem, the Konnoak Hills congregation was organized in 1950. Its original building is now part of a modern church plant. On Labor Day 1951 a service was held in a store building in the Mount Tabor section of the city. For this Messiah congregation, a building, enlarged in recent years, was opened in October 1953.

Growth Outside of Salem

While the Moravian Church was growing within the city of Winston-Salem, quite a number of new congregations came into existence in communities outside the city. Fulp and Wachovia Arbor were started in 1893, Union Cross was begun in 1895, and in the same year Willow Hill, in Virginia, was organized as an outgrowth of Mount Bethel.

In 1896 four congregations were organized. In Mayodan, Moravian services began with the laying out of the town. The erection of a new church plant began with the building of a Christian education unit in 1963. Enterprise congregation was established as a filial of Friedberg; Moravia of Kernersville. The fourth congregation is Mizpah, associated with Bethania. In 1897, the New Philadelphia congregation organized the Bethesda church. In recent years all of these congregations have enlarged their buildings.

In 1900 a congregation was organized at Clemmons, where Edwin T. Clemmons, founder of the town, had dreamed of having a Moravian church and school. For some years a high school was operated jointly by the state and our church; then the school became a public school, and its building was remodeled for Sunday school and church purposes.

In 1908 the Moravians bought a little building in the city of Greensboro as the home of the congregation they had established there. In time the congregation was able to move to a better location and on Christmas Eve 1949 a new church building was opened.

Another city church was begun in 1920 in Charlotte. In 1924, a chapel-parsonage was erected on a piece of property presented to them in the Myers Park section of the city. In November 1954 a beautiful new church, built in 1949, was dedicated. On July 15, 1962, a second Moravian church in Charlotte was opened on Park Road.

Further expansion into other North Carolina cities resulted in the formation of the Grace Moravian congregation in Mt. Airy in 1925. In 1928 the Moravians began work in Leaksville, now part of the city of Eden, not far from Mayodan.

Meanwhile other churches were springing up near the center of Winston-Salem. Advent was formed, with the help of Friedberg, from two Sunday schools one of which dated back as far as 1835. A chapel was erected here in 1897, but the congregation was not organized until 1924.

In 1931 the Rural Hall congregation was organized as the outgrowth of a Ladies' Aid Society organized eight years before. In 1932 the Moravians took over a little congregation which Henry Rippel, a Hessian soldier in the Revolutionary war, had established at Hopewell. The Lutherans were good enough to sell the little building for fifty dollars.

In October 1953 a congregation was organized in North Carolina's capital city of Raleigh, and in 1957 a building was erected on Ridge Road.

In 1960 the Southern Province expanded into Florida by establishing a congregation in the Coral Ridge area of Fort Lauderdale. Fifteen miles north, a second congregation was organized in Boca Raton in 1962. Both of these churches closed in recent years. A lasting work was established in the Orlando area at Rolling Hills in 1967. In Miami, the Prince of Peace congregation was established among Nicaraguan refugees in 1987.

Stone Mountain, a suburb of Atlanta, Georgia, was the location for a new work begun in 1975. New congregations were established in Wilmington in 1979, Lewisville in 1980, Hickory in 1983 and Kernersville in 1988, all in North Carolina; and in Richmond, Virginia, in 1987.

The Unity of the Brethren in Texas

As far back as 1850 Protestants from Bohemia and Moravia began coming to various parts of the United States. The group with which our church has had most contact is the Unity of the Brethren, in Texas. This group claims John Hus as their spiritual forebear, and has therefore a background much like our own.

In 1864 they established their first congregation at Wesley, Texas. In 1903 about twenty congregations united to form the Evangelical Unity of Czech Moravian Brethren. Today there are about thirty-five congregations. The Unity has a Hus Bible School which meets for two months every summer. They are much interested in the mission work of our church and with the Moravian Church support our Board of World Mission. Some of our ministers have served in Texas on a "loan" basis and quite a few of their pastors have studied in our seminary.

The Moravians in California

After Helen Hunt Jackson published Ramona in 1884, Americans everywhere were shocked to learn how the Indians in southern California were being exploited by unscrupulous whites. One of the many societies formed to remedy matters asked the Moravians to send missionaries into the area.

For a few years the work William H. Weinland began in 1889 showed signs of growth. The first missionaries preached in half a dozen areas, and Captain John Morongo, most influential Indian in the community, became a staunch friend and defender of the mission. But in spite of public protests, local politicians saw to it that whites were never excluded from Indian lands, so the systematic spoiling of the Native American went on.

In answer to a desire frequently expressed by Moravians in California, the Eastern District Board voted in 1952 to appropriate $25,000 for the establishment of a congregation in the Los Angeles area. The Rev. Mervin C. Weidner was sent to California. In time a desirable site was purchased in Downey, and in 1954 a congregation was organized with eighty-eight members. In 1956 a large house in Covina became the home for a second congregation, organized in May 1957; new buildings were completed in 1961.

In 1956, the Indian mission near Banning was reorganized as the third congregation in the state. Then, on November 12, 1967, ground was broken in Yorba Linda for a fourth Moravian church, and in this building the first charter members were received in December 1969.

A new area of work was established in suburban Phoenix, Arizona, in 1983 when the Morning Star congregation was organized.

Three Additional Features

Three additional features of American church life must be mentioned. The first is increasing concern for the care of the elderly. In 1928, Moravians opened a Home for the Aged at Lake Auburn, Minnesota. In 1988 this facility was relocated to Chaska, where it is joined to an apartment complex known as Talheim. In 1952 and 1958 small houses were opened in Easton and York, Pennsylvania. Then, in 1973 the Eastern District began construction of an extensive full-care facility for the aged known as Moravian Manor at Lititz, Pennsylvania, and in 1987 Moravian Hall Square Retirement Community in

Nazareth opened its doors. In 1969 the Western District began a full-care facility at Watertown, Wisconsin, known as Marquardt Village which serves 350 residents. In 1972 Southern Province Moravians completed a beautiful home for the elderly near the historic Bethabara church.

A second feature is the increasing interest in Moravian music. The Moravian Music Foundation has been instrumental in editing and publishing dozens of the anthems and instrumental compositions which made our settlement congregations famous in colonial days. When the John F. Kennedy Arts Center was opened in Washington, D.C., in 1971, a concert of Moravian music was a completely sold-out feature.

The third feature is Moravian Open Door, a housing unit for 42 elderly homeless of the city of New York, which opened its doors in 1987. The facility's goal is to provide a supporting family-like atmosphere where caring for one another can be reality. This, along with the Coffee Pot Ministry of the First Moravian congregation, exemplifies the concern which members of the church have for those whose lives reflect the needy condition of men and women of all ages.

"Lead On, O King Eternal!"

When the Rev. A. H. Mumford completed *Our Church's Story* in 1911, he wrote: " The future of our Church is with you who read the story of our Church and understand her meaning and her greatness. That story has been written in vain if it does not show you that you are heirs to a glorious past and may be fathers to a more glorious future."

Index

Other Books on Moravian History

Adams, Charles B. *Our Moravian Hymn Heritage.* Bethlehem, Pa.: Moravian Church, 1984. 152 pp. $2.00.

Fries, Adelaide L. *Customs and Practices of the Moravian Church.* Winston-Salem, N.C.: Board of Christian Education and Evangelism, 1973. 72 pp. $2.00.

Hamilton, J. Taylor, and Kenneth G. Hamilton. *History of the Moravian Church.* Bethlehem, Pa., and Winston-Salem, N.C.: Interprovincial Board of Christian Education, 1967. 724 pp. $14.95.

Michel, Bernard E. *The Belfry that Moved.* Bethlehem, Pa.: Board of Christian Education and Evangelism, 1959. 64 pp., illustrated, for children. $.75.

Rondthaler, Katherine Boring. *Tell Me a Story.* Bethlehem, Pa., and Winston-Salem, N.C.: Comenius Press, 1948. 64 pp., illustrated, for children. $5.00.

Sawyer, Edwin A. *All About the Moravians.* Bethlehem, Pa., and Winston-Salem, N.C.: Moravian Church in America, 1990. 64 pp. $4.00.

Weinlick, John R. *Count Zinzendorf.* Reprinted Bethlehem, Pa., and Winston-Salem, N.C.: Moravian Church in America, 1989. 240 pp. $8.00.

Weinlick, John R. and Albert H. Frank. *The Moravian Church through the Ages.* Bethlehem, Pa., and Winston-Salem, N.C.: Moravian Church in America, 1989. 128 pp. $6.00.

Available from

Moravian Book and Gift Shop
P.O. Box 10488, Salem Station
Winston-Salem, NC 27108
919-723-6262

Department of Publications and Communications
P. O. Box 1245
Bethlehem , PA 18016-1245
215-867-0593